ABOUT THE AUTHOR

Christopher Barnatt has been working as a futurist for over 20 years. He is Associate Professor of Computing & Future Studies in Nottingham University Business School, and the author of ExplainingTheFuture.com, ExplainingComputers. com and their associated YouTube channels. Christopher has written seven previous books and numerous articles on future studies and computing, and appears regularly in the media. You can follow him at twitter.com/ChrisBarnatt.

By the same author:

SEVEN WAYS TO FIX THE WORLD

Christopher Barnatt

ExplainingTheFuture.com

First published by ExplainingTheFuture.com

For press, rights, translation and other enquiries,
please e-mail chris@explainingthefuture.com

ISBN-10 : 1-479-24284-5

ISBN-13 : 978-1-479-24284-9

Printed and bound on demand.

Typeset in Adobe InDesign by Christopher Barnatt.

Disclaimer
While every effort has been made to ensure that the content in
this book is as accurate as possible, no warranty or fitness
is implied. All trademarks included in this book are
appropriately capitalized and no attempt is made
or implied to supersede the rights of their
respective owners.

1 3 5 7 9 10 8 6 4 2

To dreamers and shapers everywhere.

Working together, we can fix the world.

CONTENTS

ACKNOWLEDGEMENTS

This is the eighth time I have written the acknowledgements for a book. Although on this occasion things are somewhat different, as I am not just the author, but also the publisher. I therefore have no editor to thank (or blame!) for commissioning this work, and no production staff to acknowledge. I do, however, very much want to thank Howard Watson for his great copy-editing. Fingers crossed, between us we have sorted everything out.

More broadly, many people have influenced this work and my life as I have been writing. For a start I would like to thank Nicholas Browne for his ongoing medical support, and Katherine Behenna for restoring my voice after it disappeared for many months following surgery. I would also like to thank Fiona Cameron, Steve Upcraft and James Brindle for continuing to inflict me on their clients and listeners. Hopefully this book will give us even more to talk about. I would also like to thank my YouTube subscribers and Twitter followers for making that click. You all know who you are!

Back in the ivory towers of the University of Nottingham, I would like to acknowledge the support of many colleagues. These include Stephen Diacon for his good advice, Ken Starkey for the many chats in which we try to keep each other sane, Sue Tempest for reminding me how and when I write best, Teresa Bee for extending her counselling role beyond the students, and Chris Bates, Tracey Bettinson,

Thomas Chesney, Sally Hopkinson, George Kuk, Steve Moore, Gina Rogers, Duncan Shaw, Rozina Shaikh, Kieran Woodward and Victoria Wrigley for generally putting up with me and allowing me to bounce crazy ideas around.

Finally, I would like to thank my parents for too many things to try and list, as well as Mark Daintree and Margaret Hiscox for their ongoing support over many, many years.

PROLOGUE

As the title of this book implies, the world is broken and needs to be fixed. Many people are aware of this, although relatively few are doing anything about it. Not least, the vast majority of our political and business 'leaders' continue to bury their heads in the proverbial sand in the hope that the status quo will last them out. Nevertheless, as the situation deteriorates, it is going to become more and more obvious that we cannot go on living quite as we do today.

So what exactly is the matter? Well for a start, human civilization is continuing to expand far beyond the nurturing capacity of its mother planet. Within a few decades, we will therefore face biting shortages of energy, food and fresh water. Climate change also demands our attention, while mass consumer culture is leading us to ruin. On top of all this, the dominant religion of the 20th century – economics – has started to seriously fail us all as an appropriate resource allocation mechanism. Other systems of belief and connection are also running dry, with a large number of people now isolated not just from the natural world, but from each other.

In response to these grand challenges, this book is a positive manifesto for building a better future. Admittedly, part of this Prologue will detail the starkness of our situation. Yet nowhere herein is it my intention to spread doom and gloom. Nor am I going to point fingers and apportion blame. Whether any individual, organization or nation is part of the problem or part of the solution has to be judged not on their activities in a different age, but on the basis of their intentions and actions from this day forward. Every one of us will make an impact on the world of tomorrow. The choice before us all is simply whether we want our legacy to help or hinder those to come.

In the second half of the 20th century, raping the future to sustain the present somehow became socially and culturally acceptable. But this practice cannot go on indefinitely. For many decades a great deal of economic growth has been achieved by robbing future humanity of many of the basic necessities of living. And if this does not stop pretty soon it will be too late to make amends.

Given today's widespread addiction to short-term consumerism, fixing the world is not going to be easy. But then nothing that is worth doing ever is. As soon as there are explicit and viable options on the table, it is also likely that many people will be willing to help build a better future. Once a reasonable momentum is established, fixing the world will therefore not have to be left to an idealistic minority.

OUR CHALLENGES AHEAD

As I have already stated, I have no intention of doom mongering. Yet to make explicit why we need to fix the world, it is essential to at least briefly outline the seriousness of our situation. The following therefore provides an overview of the most pressing challenges we now face. For the interested – or the alarmed – more information can be found on my website ExplainingTheFuture.com, or in my previous book *25 Things You Need to Know About the Future*.[1]

PEAK OIL

The biggest challenge on the near-term horizon is the end of our petroleum-based economy. Reliable estimates suggest that proven global oil reserves will last until about 2057.[2] It is, however, the much more pressing matter of Peak Oil that has to demand our immediate attention.

The basic problem is that we continue to consume oil reserves faster than we discover new ones. Peak Oil subsequently refers to the point in time when global oil production will reach its maximum, and after which it will start to decline. This situation is illustrated in the approximated 'bell curve' for global oil production shown in Prologue Figure 1.

After Peak Oil is reached, there will be an ever-widening gap between oil demand and oil supply. As a result, oil will inevitably start to become scarcer and more expensive. The implications will include a rise in the price of oil-fuelled transportation, as well as an increase in the price and a decrease in availability of all products that use oil in their production. The latter include not just traditional plastics and synthetic fabrics, but also most agricultural produce. We may not currently sit at the dinner table directly ingesting petroleum. But most of us do rely on oil to kill the pests that threaten our crops. We are currently also very dependent on oil to cultivate, harvest, package and transport a great deal of our food.

Exactly when Peak Oil will occur is unknown and remains a matter of significant debate. So-called 'early toppers' – such as the UK government's former chief scientist Sir David King – believe that demand for oil may start outstripping supply as early as 2014. At the other end of the spectrum, some 'late toppers' believe that Peak Oil will not occur until at least 2030. To try and bring some clarity to the situation, in 2009 the UK Energy Research Centre published a weighty report based on a review of over 500 studies, an analysis of industry databases, and a comparison of 14 global supply forecasts. This noted that 'sufficient information is available to allow the status and risk of global oil depletion to be

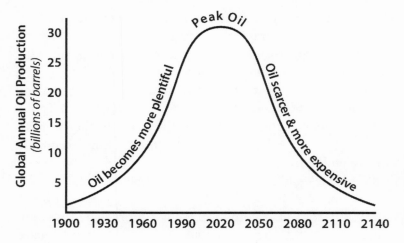

Prologue Figure 1: The Peak Oil Curve

adequately assessed'. The report subsequently concluded that 'a peak in conventional oil production before 2030 appears likely and there is a significant risk of a peak before 2020'.[3]

CLIMATE CHANGE

The fact that the Earth is heating up due to an accumulation of greenhouse gasses in the atmosphere is now widely accepted. Admittedly, the speed and impact of this warming, together with humanity's role in making it happen, remain a matter of considerable debate. Yet no major government now denies the existence of climate change. All of us will therefore be affected not just by a changing climate, but in addition by those political and economic actions increasingly being taken to try and limit the future heating of the globe.

According to the Intergovernmental Panel on Climate Change (IPCC), by 2100 average global temperatures will rise by somewhere between 1.1°C and 6.4°C. While this may not sound like much, even two degrees of warming is likely to decrease crop yields across southern Europe by 20 per cent, have a similar impact on rice production across Asia, and lead to the extinction of up to 40 per cent of species on the planet. Increases in average global temperatures will also further melt glaciers and raise sea levels. The IPCC has calculated that our oceans will rise by between 18 and 59 cm by 2100. In the coming decades, hundreds of millions of people will therefore face significant flooding risks. Later this century, great metropolises including London, Shanghai, New York and Tokyo are also likely to be under threat.

Some level of global warming is now irrevocably baked-in to our planetary system. The IPCC and most other informed parties therefore advise that our challenge is to try and limit the temperature increase to no more than 2°C. This would probably require carbon dioxide and other greenhouse gas emissions to peak this decade or early next, and to fall to 60 per cent of their current levels by 2050. This clearly presents a very major challenge and requires urgent action.

Some reputable commentators also caution that the IPCC could be seriously underestimating the severity of near-future climate change due to its over-reliance on computer simulations of the atmosphere. Most notably, renowned climate scientist James Lovelock has repeatedly warned that actual climate measurements already show a far greater level of global warming than the IPCC's computer models continue to predict. Worse still, Lovelock points out that by reducing the industrial emission of greenhouse gasses, we may rapidly reduce those layers of pollution that are currently preventing the Earth from warming even faster.[4] According to the National Center for Atmospheric Research (NCAR) in the United States, the Earth's deepest oceans may also at present be absorbing enough heat to conceal the true extent of global warming for up to a decade.[5]

PEAK WATER

Partially as a consequence of climate change, in the next few decades adequate supplies of fresh water will also be under threat. In fact, according to the United Nations, 'by 2025, 1.8 billion people will be living in countries or regions with absolute water scarcity', while two-thirds of the world's population will face stressed or restricted water supplies.[6]

Given that the majority of the Earth's surface is covered by water, many people find it difficult to believe that water scarcity presents a significant future challenge. The problem is that, even though our planet is blessed with about 326 quintillion gallons of water, around 97 per cent of this is salty and unsuitable for agricultural use or direct human consumption.

Most fresh water is also frozen in the polar ice caps or inaccessible very deep underground. While the lakes, underground aquifers and other fresh water reserves that we can use are still quite large, they have a pretty fixed rate of replenishment. Many fresh water reserves are also already being drained well beyond this natural replenishment level. As a result, many parts of the world will soon face a 'Peak Water' situation where demand starts to consistently outstrip available local supply.

Within a decade or so, groundwater production peaks are likely to become a major concern in many countries including China, India, Israel, Mexico, Saudi Arabia, Spain and the United States. In fact, around half of the world's population now lives in regions where the water table is falling. Climate change is in addition causing lakes to evaporate more quickly, as well as threatening glaciers such as those in the Himalayas that feed many major rivers in China.

Because fresh water reserves are very unevenly distributed, different parts of the world will be affected by Peak Water at different times and in different ways. In traditionally drought-plagued regions like parts of Africa, humanitarian catastrophes loom as millions will not have enough water to drink. Across far wider parts of the globe, drinking water is unlikely to be under threat, but agricultural yields will be reduced due to a lack of sufficient water for irrigation.

In some parts of the world, water scarcity is set to force industrial relocation. For example, water-intensive industries in the United States will probably have to move from the increasingly dry south west to the Great Lakes region. Even countries with pretty robust water supplies like the United Kingdom will sooner-or-later feel the impact of Peak Water as supplies of imported food products dwindle. Many European supermarkets currently stock their shelves with fruit and vegetables grown in water-challenged countries including Ethiopia, India and South Africa. How long this can continue – both practically and ethically – must soon be seriously questioned.

FOOD SHORTAGES

The 'perfect storm' of Peak Oil, climate change and Peak Water will additionally put pressure on global food supplies. Already, due to rising temperatures, water shortages and soil erosion, average harvests of grain and rice are falling in many regions. As petroleum becomes scarcer and more expensive, the use of oil-based pesticides and oil-fuelled farm machinery will also be constrained.

As China and other nations rapidly industrialize, the proportion of meat in the average human diet is also increasing. This is problematic because diets that are rich in meat are more resource intensive. At present, in a poorer nation like India the average diet requires less than 200 kg of grain to be harvested per person per year. In contrast, in the United States around 800 kg has to be harvested, with the majority fed to animals that are later eaten by humans.[7]

It is difficult to argue against the right of developing nations to industrialize. Even so, there is simply not enough conventional farm land on the planet to permit all of humanity to eat a meat-rich diet like that currently enjoyed across the West. As demand for meat continues to grow, supplies are therefore going to become relatively scarce and more expensive.

Food shortages are also likely to be heightened as land is diverted for non-food agriculture. Already vast quantities of corn, rape, sugar cane and other crops are being harvested to produce biofuels and bioplastics. In time, these more eco-friendly products may be able to be produced from agricultural waste or synthetically engineered algae. But until such third-generation petroleum alternatives become viable, every acre used to cultivate a biocrop is inevitably an acre removed from food production.

In the coming decades, the quantity of food we can obtain from the oceans will also fall rather than rise. Many groups of scientists have confirmed a serious decline in marine life, with three-quarters of fish stocks already being fished at or beyond their natural rate of replenishment. Indeed, in 2010 the ten-year Census of Marine Life reported that commercial fishing on a global scale will collapse entirely by 2050 unless drastic action is taken.[8]

BROADER RESOURCE DEPLETION

Almost inevitably, the constant expansion and industrialization of humanity will place intense pressures not just on supplies of water, food and oil, but on all raw materials. A 2011 report from the United Nations Environment Programme (UNEP) calculated that, if nothing is done, humanity's demand for natural resources will rise to around 140 billion tonnes of minerals, ores, fossil fuels and biomass every year by 2050.[9] Equivalent to almost three times our current rate of resource consumption, this is way beyond what can be sustained.

Over the past 40 years, a set of studies carried out at the Massachusetts Institute of Technology (MIT) has made our situation pretty explicit. The first of these was published in 1972 and called *The Limits to Growth*.[10] This was followed by a 20-year update *Beyond the Limits to Growth*,[11] and *Limits to Growth: The 30-Year Update*.[12]

The team behind *The Limits to Growth* has repeatedly warned that humanity has an ecological footprint greater than the Earth can sustain. The stark implication of this fact is that our civilization will inevitably collapse if we do not reduce global consumption levels.

Back in 1972, it was predicted that we had about half a century to change our ways. Unfortunately we have done very little, which means that we now have at most one or two decades to try and prevent our slow decline. We therefore need to urgently figure out how to achieve more with less. Or, as the aforementioned UNEP report neatly put it, we have to find ways to 'uncouple' natural resource usage from economic growth.

Unless we quite rapidly change our ways, we will soon career into a global state of 'Peak Everything'. For example, fresh supplies of critical metals including zinc, tantalum, antimony, indium, gallium and even copper could be entirely depleted by 2050. Significant shortages of these materials are also likely well before that, with prices set to rise as a result. Already the price of indium – an essential raw material used in the production of LCD displays – has risen from $40 per kilogram in 2003 to over $600. Like it or not, we cannot go on consuming natural resources in the way we do today.

POPULATION EXPANSION

Underlying all of the above challenges is the pressure on the Earth caused by a significantly expanding human population. Every year there are tens of millions more human beings to feed, clothe and shelter, with a significant proportion of them likely to demand a smartphone, a vehicle and regular air travel. Such a situation is of course unsustainable.

Around 2,000 years ago there were a mere 100 million human beings on Planet Earth. Were there still that number today, none of the aforementioned challenges would be an issue. But there are actually now around seven billion people alive, with eight billion expected by 2030 and more than nine billion by 2050. Pretty soon something will therefore have to give.

I am a pretty strong believer in the ability of the human race to invent and apply new technologies to solve apparently insurmountable problems. That is, after all, how we have survived for so long and risen to planetary dominance. In the future we may be able to use genetic engineering to increase food production, to transition to electric transportation, to develop wind, wave and solar power, and to do all sorts of other more resource efficient technological things. Even so, short of a mass future migration into space, there is no long-term technological fix to the problem of over population. In fact, technological advances that continue to extend the human lifespan are likely to more than cancel out the help that technology may render on this frontier.

Of all the challenges on the horizon, population expansion may be the most difficult to address. This is because there can be only one pretty unpalatable solution, and that is for less people to live on Planet Earth. Many futurists believe that, by the end of this century, an optimal and sustainable human population will be no more than a couple of billion. And unfortunately they may well be right.

Any rapid transition to a world with perhaps one-quarter of its current population would obviously have major humanitarian implications. We therefore have to hope that, if a mass depopulation is our destiny, we will slowly and naturally transition to a less populated planet over a very significant period of time.

THE END OF ECONOMIC GROWTH

Our final grand challenge is to wean ourselves away from an assumed requirement for year-on-year economic growth. Just as a constantly expanding population is unsustainable on a single planet with fixed resources, so too is a constantly expanding economy. We also have no need to constantly consume more and more.

When a baby exits the womb, nobody expects the poor infant to physically expand outwards and upwards indefinitely until they die. Rather, we anticipate a period of natural growth that ceases when the child has matured into an adult. There may now be a tendency for some individuals to continue to physically expand until their obesity kills them. But that is neither a natural nor desirable situation.

Economies – like people – can and should mature to become big and wealthy enough. For several centuries economists have made us believe that constant economic growth is necessary because they have also conned us into never paying our way. Indeed, for decades governments have borrowed recklessly on the assumption that, by the time their bonds mature and have to be repaid, years of economic growth and inflation will have significantly reduced their real value. The problem is, on a planet now facing all of the aforementioned challenges, this strategy is no longer viable.

For too long the citizens of this planet have served economics and economic growth, rather than being served by the systems of resource allocation and administration that are supposed to serve us. To a large extent, redressing the balance is what this book is all about.

SEVEN FUTURE SOLUTIONS

Over the past 50 years, human civilization has started to focus far too heavily on short-term decadence, and far too little on long-term survival. Not least, we have come to place the welfare of the economy above the health of the biosphere that keeps us alive. At a species level, this is nothing less than suicidal. Or to cite the opening of the *Warning to Humanity* signed by over 1,500 leading scientists and Nobel laureates on 18th November 1992:

> Human beings and the natural world are on a collision course. Human activities inflict harsh and often irreversible damage on the environment and on critical resources. If not checked, many of our current practices put at serious risk the future that we wish for human society and the plant and animal kingdoms, and may so alter the living world that it will be unable to sustain life in the manner that we know. Fundamental changes are urgent if we are to avoid the collision our present course will bring about.[13]

I could continue for tens or even hundreds of pages to provide a great many more stark, poetic and powerful indictments of our sorry situation. Many books have indeed been written that do this very well. This said, while spreading an awareness of our precarious situation is valuable, pragmatically it is far more important to start figuring out what we can do about it. Fixing rather than describing the world is after all the focus of this book. So let me now introduce you to the seven, interrelated things that I think we all need to start focusing on.

MORE LOCAL LIVING

The first way to fix the world is to consume more local produce and to work and play far closer to home. This need not imply that we all have to go back to living in tiny hamlets in complete isolation from the modern plague of globalization. Yet it cannot be sensible for us to continue to constantly favour food and other products that are produced hundreds or thousands of miles from where we live. Similarly, the mass transportation of people to remote workplaces is a modern ritual that we can no longer afford to practise. Chapter 1 will therefore look at a range of options for more local living. These include a re-balancing of globalization, the establishment of urban agriculture, technological developments that will facilitate more local manufacturing, and opportunities for more people to work from home.

LOW ENERGY LIFESTYLES

As well as living more locally, in the fairly near future we will all have to consume less energy. Already significant investments are being made in wind, wave and solar power. However, because no alternative energy source can deliver the quantity of energy that we currently obtain from petroleum and other fossil fuels, reducing our energy requirement is going to be essential over the next couple of decades. To this end, chapter 2 reviews the pending 'net energy time bomb'. It then examines the development of low power devices, as well as those steps that will need to be taken to enable our transition to less energy-intensive lifestyles.

DEMATERIALIZATION

OK, so you may have read the word 'dematerialization' and thought of a brightly clad *Star Trek* crew member beaming down to an alien planet. Here, however, I am using the word to refer to a migration toward activities that are less reliant on the consumption of physical resources.

In part, dematerialization is dependent on more local living and low energy lifestyles. But it will also require us to do some things less or not at all, and to achieve other things in new ways.

Over the past decade, the Internet has allowed us to produce and communicate digital information far more, while manufacturing and transporting atom-based things somewhat less. With many people now downloading music and obtaining their news, books and video entertainment online, dematerialization has therefore already begun to happen.

New technologies such as 3D printing will soon also allow dematerialization to be taken to the next level. Even so, as I shall argue in chapter 3, we still need to develop a radically new relationship with things. If this can be achieved – and the whole ethos of our consumer society starts to be seriously questioned – then a new 'gentler mode of capitalism' may even emerge.

DESIGN FOR REPAIR

Another way to reduce our consumption of both energy and physical resources is design for repair. This will facilitate a return to an age in which most products are mended rather than discarded when they go wrong. Over the past half century, the production of things that can be repaired has sadly become unfashionable, with constant disposal and product replacement strongly encouraged at a cultural level. Chapter 4 therefore focuses on what needs to be done to reverse this trend, and to return human society to an age in which most people discard things less and value things more.

CROWDSOURCING

Fixing the world will require the collective talents of mass humanity. Mechanisms for effectively generating and sharing knowledge among thousands and even millions of people will therefore be needed in spades. For the majority of recorded history, bringing together very large numbers of human beings to work on great undertakings has only been achieved under conditions of dictatorship or mass bureaucracy. Yet with the rise of the Internet there is now another way.

Crowdsourcing is where online technologies are used to generate value from the activities of a great many people. Web pioneer Tim O'Reilly has long heralded the power of the Internet to harness collective intelligence, and this practice is now seriously taking hold.[14] Indeed, as we shall see in chapter 5, tens of thousands of global strangers are already pioneering the use of collaborative online tools to create new 'open source' products that traditional businesses will not or cannot deliver. Community is therefore already beginning to trump competition, while work is starting to be obtained and allocated in new ways.

MORE WOMEN IN AUTHORITY

Just over half of the human beings on this planet are women. Yet look around most boardrooms and parliaments and you would not know it. As we are all aware, women remain significantly under-represented at high levels in most organizations. In some supposedly 'advanced' cultures and religions, women are still even treated as second-class citizens. As a consequence, the majority of the big decisions that drive and shape human civilization continue to be made by only one half of our gene pool.

Two of the key things that we need more of on this planet – community building and cooperation – involve the application of skills that females typically possess and practise more naturally than males. To fix the world, we therefore need more women in authority as a genetic counter-balance to male-dominated decision making. Some researchers have even indicated that the scandalous risk taking that resulted in the credit crunch of 2008 was testosterone fuelled.[15] Lehman Sisters may indeed not have got into the same mess as Lehman Brothers. Chapter 6 subsequently assesses how we may all benefit from the introduction of a majority female perspective into humanity's decision making mechanisms. It also considers how this may actually be achieved.

THE DEATH OF ECONOMICS

John Maynard Keynes, the guru of modern economics, once stated that 'in the long run we are all dead'. It is therefore perhaps not surprising that most economists to this day continue to almost completely ignore pollution, resource depletion, the destruction of the biosphere, and many of the other consequences of modern business activity. And yet, it remains obvious to the rest of us that in the long run our children and their children will still be very much alive. All of our children and their descendants will also be cursed with our folly if we do not choose to mend our collective ways, and to start taking at least some responsibility for tomorrow.

To live above a very basic subsistence level, human beings require more than systems of barter. Financial services organizations and a modern economy are therefore a prerequisite for the survival of industrial civilization. In calling for the death of economics, I am therefore not suggesting that all economic practices and associated logic should be discarded. Rather, what I am signalling is that we should cease to rely quite so heavily on economics as the driving engine of human civilization.

Most of the really important decisions made by an individual in their lifetime are not made according to the rules of economics (although I know many economists who could show me dubious and complex equations to dispute that claim!). So why should we expect the big decisions that drive wider civilization to always be taken on economic grounds? The use of economic logic did not drive humanity to build pyramids and cathedrals, to land on the Moon, or to go to war to prevent genocide. Increasingly, economics has obtained a stranglehold on our common sense, and this is something that needs to be addressed.

In recent decades, too great a global belief in economic logic has resulted in excessive globalization. Economic exuberance has also failed to cost the full implications of our high-energy, oil-saturated lifestyles; has fuelled our lust for materialized living; has propagated a disposable culture; has promoted competition over cooperation; and has even made us value far too highly testosterone-fuelled male management egos. OK, so if you were counting, you will have noticed that I have now linked decreasing our reliance on economics to all six of my other ways to fix the world. This ought also to be expected. Economics currently dominates our collective consciousness. If we are to fix the world – and we have to – then economics must be put firmly back in its place as just one of the many tools that we use to progress and maintain our civilization.

* * *

FOUNDATIONS FOR TOMORROW

In the first half of this Prologue I highlighted some pretty major, planetary-scale problems. To explain why we need to fix the world this was absolutely necessary. But I am also mindful that such a list of challenges may lead some people to believe that no individual action can make a difference. It is therefore important to stress that every one of our actions really matters a great deal.

There can be no escaping the fact that every one of us is now part of the problem or part of the solution. While any one individual action may on the surface appear inconsequential, our *collective actions* inevitably and rapidly aggregate. This means that any actions we may individually take to improve our situation are important. Further, by deciding and acting to help build a better future, we may all inspire others to do the same.

Finally before I finish this Prologue, I need to make a couple of things absolutely explicit. For a start, I have to acknowledge that I am writing from a highly privileged, developed nation perspective. We should never forget that over a billion people still go to sleep hungry, and that most citizens of this planet cannot obtain clean water from a tap. For billions of people, the challenges of tomorrow that this book seeks to address may therefore be far less significant than those current problems with which they have to contend every single day.

For those whose lives have been blighted by the financial crisis and related austerity, fixing the world of tomorrow may also seem like a secondary concern. Noting these facts, I can only argue that the more we do to try and address our most pressing future challenges, the better it may be not just for future humanity, but for all of those people who currently live in less blessed regions of the globe or who are otherwise suffering current hardship.

I also want to acknowledge that one little book cannot actually hope to fix the world. Each of the following seven chapters will provide some ideas that individuals and individual organizations could readily embrace to start making a difference. Even so, this work can at best constitute just one tiny element of a much wider debate concerning how we may collectively win against the odds in the decades ahead.

All of us need to recognize that the future will not just happen. Or at least, it will only 'just happen' for some people if they let others do it for them or to them. More than anything, fixing the world is about taking control of the future – and that is something in which we must all take a hand. To survive and thrive, humanity must learn to consume less while achieving more. To do this we will all increasingly have to act with others in mind – be they fellow citizens today, or the inhabitants of tomorrow.

1

MORE LOCAL LIVING

From the beginning of modern agriculture to a few centuries ago, most people rarely travelled very far from home. Granted, a few soldiers, sailors, merchants and explorers did journey great distances and even travelled the globe. The exploits of these far more mobile individuals also dominate our history books. But for the vast majority of the population, long-distance travel was a logistical impossibility.

In the age when few people travelled, relatively few things did either. Some high value items – including precious metals, exotic fabrics, works of art and spices – were carried across land and sea by merchants. Monarchs and others who commanded great wealth could sometimes also afford to import other goods from far, far away. But aside from these rare exceptions, the vast majority of most people's food, clothing and everyday possessions had to be sourced locally.

As the world industrialized, both people and things started to become far more mobile. Canals and then railways allowed perishable items to be consumed far from their place of origin. Across the 20th century, oil-fuelled transportation subsequently permitted a truly global economy to emerge. Indeed today, food, natural resources, components and finished goods are transported around the planet so ubiquitously that many items are the product of scores of nations.

The combined parts of many products have sometimes even travelled tens of thousands of miles before they come into our possession.

The mass transportation of physical things from region to region and country to country has become a mainstay of modern civilization. As a result, it is likely that most people in developed nations purchase few if any items that are grown or manufactured entirely from local resources. Unfortunately, in the face of Peak Oil, climate change, resource depletion, and those other challenges outlined in the Prologue, this cannot go on for much longer. This chapter therefore discusses why and how we will increasingly have to live more locally.

THE RISE OF GLOBALIZATION

When I was at school the word 'globalization' was just entering common usage. In fact, I very clearly remember my economics teacher excitedly explaining how it was a great idea for nations to specialize in those activities in which they had 'comparative advantage'. What this meant in practice was that if countries in Asia could make things cheaper than we could in the United Kingdom, then we should be jolly thankful and let our home manufacturing industries die. If we wanted to become dependent on food grown right around the world, then this too was fine so long as the price was right.

Today, as in my childhood, the fact that globalization requires vast quantities of resources to be used to transport things around the planet is still not widely recognized as a problem. After all, why should people in London eat fruit grown in the Garden of England when cheaper apples can be imported from South Africa and blueberries can be flown in from the United States?

I personally find it most alarming that the folly of mass global trade is still not widely recognized. Yet whether people want to accept it or not, transporting a large volume of materials around the planet will soon become increasingly problematic. In resource utilization terms, it in fact never made sense. While in the past half century the world may have shrunk, this feat has only been achieved by shrinking our reserves of fossil fuels to a far greater and entirely unrepeatable extent.

The challenge we now face is establishing a new mode of globalization that balances the current advantages of international trade with the resource savings that we need to reap from more local living. Despite what some extreme environmentalists may preach, the rise of a fluidly-functioning global economy has brought many benefits that we would be foolish to entirely discard. For a start, globalization has helped many less developed regions to industrialize. Pressures to trade globally also helped to bring down the Iron Curtain, and even persuaded China to open its borders with the rest of the world. The fact that mass humanity is nowhere near as divided as it was 50 years ago has to be a good thing. We therefore need to maintain today's level of global integration as we in tandem seek ways to consume fewer globally-sourced things.

GLOBAL & LOCAL SOURCING

It will probably continue to make sense for many nations to import at least some varieties of agricultural produce – such as cotton, tea or bananas – that cannot easily be grown in their local climate. Many metal and mineral deposits are also far richer in some regions of the world than others, in turn making their continued transportation from one nation to another a practical inevitability. These exceptions noted, in resource terms it is going to become far more difficult to justify sourcing any item globally if a reasonable local substitute is available or could readily be made so.

Working out which things ought to be sourced locally rather than globally will require us to stop making production and purchase decisions entirely on the basis of monetary price. Instead, we need to start considering very carefully the entire *resource envelope* that the production and acquisition of any item involves. To this end, it is important to appreciate that the production and trade of any physical item usually consumes natural resources in three distinct ways.

Firstly, any item will use up some *raw materials and energy* as it is grown or manufactured. Many of these resources – such as the metals or plastics used to make many consumer goods – end up as part of the final product. Others, including power generated from fossil fuels, basic chemicals, or the water and grain fed to animals, are transformed into the product or otherwise spent during its production as part of an industrial or agricultural process.

Secondly, all goods indirectly consume at least some *capital resources*. For example, any item produced in a factory is indirectly responsible for the consumption of some of the energy and raw materials used to build the factory and its machinery in the first place. Even basic food items grown organically incur a tiny capital resource cost associated with the production of the tools used to work the land and to harvest them.

Finally, any item not made on a kitchen table will consume at least some *transportation resources* (and most usually oil) on its journey to its place of consumption. The raw materials used in making any item are also themselves very likely to have consumed further transportation resources to get them to the location in which an item is manufactured or grown.

Most items will consume roughly the same quantity of raw materials and energy regardless of where they are produced. When deciding which items should be sourced locally and which it is still sensible to trade globally, we should therefore largely focus on the balance of capital and transportation resources that a delivered product consumes. In turn, we may quickly conclude that we should seek a local substitute whenever the transportation resources devoted to a delivered item exceed the capital resources that it indirectly consumes.

FROM POTATOES TO MICROCHIPS

To make the above point clear, let us consider a couple of examples. At one end of the scale, and as I have already implied, shipping most fruit, vegetable and animal products around the planet is just not sensible. In fact, to import apples, potatoes, carrots and all manner of foods into the rich, green lands of the United Kingdom is nothing short of ridiculous. The capital investment required to grow most food stuffs is minimal, as any fertile piece of land can easily be converted into a traditional farm. In contrast, the transportation resources that have to be invested to move farmed produce thousands of miles are very significant. It really is daft to burn up so much oil and other resources fuelling ships or aircraft crammed full of fruit and vegetables that could usually be grown far, far closer to their point of final consumption.

At the other end of the spectrum, consider the production of microprocessors. Today these are manufactured in very few countries and shipped right around the world. This also makes perfect sense as the transportation resources required to move around a microprocessor are minimal compared to the capital resources that have to be invested to manufacture the chip in the first place.

Microprocessor fabrication plants cost billions of dollars to construct and have a relatively limited lifespan as technologies change. As many people are aware, a phenomenon called Moore's Law states that the number of transistors on a microprocessor – and hence raw microprocessor power – doubles every 18 months. There is, however, a very significant addendum to this long proven observation. This is known as Rock's Law and tells us that, as a consequence of Moore's Law, the cost of the capital equipment required to manufacture semiconductors will double every four years. In no small part this is due to the resources that have to be invested to build filtration systems capable of stopping smaller and smaller bits of dust from entering a fabrication plant. Intel, for example, recently spent $8 billion upgrading its fabrication facilities to produce its next generation of chips. We therefore need to build as few microprocessor fabrication plants as possible, so making the exploitation of global economies of scale extremely resource efficient.

To provide a few rough figures, a fabrication plant that costs around $10 billion to construct may make say 200 million chips in its lifetime. This means that each chip manufactured in it indirectly consumes $50 of capital resources (and probably far more given that the environmental costs of building an industrial plant are seldom captured in monetary terms). It may also be impossible to build a new fabrication plant to manufacture the same chips for less than $10 billion. Hence, if we were to stop globally trading in microprocessors and instead build fabrication plants in every country, the capital resources invested per microprocessor would skyrocket. They would also far outweigh the transportation resources that have to be invested to move microprocessors around the planet.

What the previous few paragraphs tell us is that trading globally in small, complex-to-manufacture items is a good idea, while trading globally in bulky, simple-to-produce items is a lot less sensible. In some instances the situation is admittedly less clear-cut, as some simple-to-produce items are manufactured from raw materials or components that are located or produced close to their current point of global manufacture. There are, however, still a very large number of situations where the transportation resource costs of globally traded items are high and yet their capital resource costs are low. One key way to fix the world is therefore to curtail global trade in favour of sourcing goods locally in as many of these situations as possible. In practice this means that we will increasingly need to obtain far more of our food, clothing, fuel, basic homewares and building materials on a local basis.

WHY THE ECONOMISTS ARE WRONG

Just before we look at some specific opportunities for more local living, it is worth pointing out that most economists would argue that my above analysis is incorrect. As they would gleefully 'prove' with curves and equations, a mass global trade in as many things as possible is highly beneficial for everybody.

There are two reasons why most economists believe mass global trade to be very positive and why I do not. Both of these reasons relate to just one key element ignored in each of our respective analyses. The thing that most economists ignore is that we do not have an infinite supply of natural resources and a biosphere that will remain healthy regardless of what industrial civilization throws at it. On the other side of the globalization argument, what I am choosing to ignore is the key role that has been played by relative labour costs in driving the rise and spread of globalization. The reason that I have ignored relative labour costs is also directly linked to the fact that natural resources are not infinite, with mass global trade soon to become unsustainable.

In a recent documentary, BBC correspondent Evan Davis told a highly plausible and compelling tale to explain high and increasing levels of global trade.[16] As he merrily proclaimed, the UK economy's migration into 'more lucrative, high value sectors' has been the right direction for Britain to have taken. According to Evan (and a whole host of traditional economic logic), even if developed countries like the UK are still capable of doing 'low value' things like growing food and making clothes, it is better for us to cease doing them if overseas labour can be exploited to do these things at lower cost.

What traditional economic logic ignores is that shifting production overseas increases the transportation resource cost of any final item delivered to the end-consumer. As we have seen, if such costs can be outweighed by capital investment savings, then globalization remains a good idea. But the infrastructure resources that have to be invested in food, clothing and most other types of 'low value' production are generally quite low, with incurred resource costs in transportation pretty high. For economists this is irrelevant if the monetary costs for a product's global transportation are smaller than the wages saved by exporting its manufacture overseas. Yet unfortunately the monetary price of transportation currently in no way reflects its true long-term environmental cost. And even if it did, the looming spectre of Peak Oil and wider resource depletion will make transporting things between nations significantly more expensive over the next few decades. As this occurs, even economists may begin to realize that any developed nation that shifts the production of necessities like food and clothing to far away lands is playing a very dangerous game.

As all nations choose – or are forced – to undertake more local manufacture and agriculture, so there will inevitably be serious implications for those countries to which global, low-cost production has increasingly been outsourced. We must not, however, fall into the trap of believing that globalization has to be maintained either for its own sake or for the short-term welfare of such nations. For the planet and humanity as a whole, it would be far better if many developing nations built fewer export production facilities and focused on the restoration and maintenance of natural ecosystems like rain forests. What the world therefore needs are new financial mechanisms that pay developing nations to care for the planet on behalf of mass humanity as global trade recedes.

This suggestion may well sound like a pipe dream and may indeed be so. Yet regardless of whether it can be achieved, dwindling natural resources and rising transportation costs will significantly reduce levels of global trade by 2020 or 2030 at the very latest. In most parts of the world, more local living is going to become the new normal whether we want it to or not. The only real choice is how we manage the transition from our current global ways.

MORE LOCAL AGRICULTURE

Burning oil to ship food around the world when it could be grown on our doorstep is nothing short of scandalous. Worse, it is downright dangerous for any region or nation to become dependent on a mechanism for food supply that cannot be sustained. Several thousand years ago, the Mayan empires fell when the fertility of the tropical soils on which they relied could no longer support their increasingly intensive farming methods. Indeed, across history, no empire or civilization has survived when it ceased to be able to feed itself.

Local food production was the bedrock of all early civilizations, and this is a state of the world to which we will fairly soon have to return. In fact, over the next few decades, most nations will have to start growing the majority of their own food.

In the face of Peak Oil, many local regions and even single cities will probably also have to embrace some level of agricultural self-reliance. It is therefore fortunate that a few influential advocates of urban food production are already figuring out how this may be achieved. These include an incredible gentleman called Dickson Despommier who believes that we need to build 'vertical farms' in the hearts of our cities.

Vertical farms are future skyscrapers in which we may grow food and raise animals. We may also develop high-rise urban agriculture to cultivate non-food crops from which we will be able to produce biofuels, bioplastics and other petroleum substitutes.

When most people first hear of vertical farming they usually dismiss the idea as ludicrous. After all, how could any form of produce be grown in a high-rise building? Where would the light come from? Or the water and perhaps the heat? And how could farming locally in a city building ever be economic?

To all of the above Dickson Despommier has an answer. In his groundbreaking book *The Vertical Farm*, he explains in detail how there is 'already a worldwide critical mass of political will, social acceptance, clever engineering, great designs, and science-based controlled environment agriculture to coalesce the concept of vertical farming into a highly efficient food-producing building'.[17]

For a start, growing food in vertical farms will allow all-year-round harvests with no weather-related crop failures. Sunlight could be directed around largely transparent buildings using mirrors and fibre-optics, with new forms of narrow-frequency LED lighting providing additional, low-energy illumination where required. Within controlled indoor environments, plants could also be grown without pesticides using hydroponic or even aeroponic agricultural techniques. The latter position small nozzles under plants to spray a nutrient-laden mist on to their roots, so reducing water consumption compared to traditional farming by at least 95 per cent. It may even be possible for the plants in some future vertical farms to help purify waste water back into drinking water, so helping cities to become more self-sufficient in their wider water and power requirements.

Vertical farming clearly has the potential to massively reduce the distance that food needs to be transported. 'On-the-vine' inventory may even become a possibility, in turn curtailing the requirement for food to be stored and often frozen on a very large scale. Petroleum could therefore be taken out of the food chain entirely for some city dwellers, with the amount of travel between where a vegetable is grown and the plate on which it is served being reduced to blocks, not miles.

If Despommier is right, vertical farms may be 20 or 30 times more productive per acre of land than conventional farms. In turn this could make them an economically viable proposition in at least some cities, and especially as petroleum prices rise. Despommier and others estimate that individual vertical farms may be capable of feeding thousands or even tens of thousands of people. As towering centre-pieces of the local community, they could also become a focus for urban regeneration, with many citizens willing to become part-time farmhands. Indeed, as Despommier hopes, with vertical farms scattered throughout the urban landscape, future city dwellers may actually start to re-embrace the ecological essentials of living.

Already, a former meatpacking plant and slaughterhouse in Chicago's Union Stock Yards is being converted into a self-sustaining vertical farm called 'The Plant'. The intention is to create a 'net-zero waste' ecosystem within the facility, with the waste from one growing space becoming the raw material for another. To this end, tenants already include a tilapia fish farm, the waste from which is being used to feed a mushroom garden and a hydroponic vegetable garden. The plants in the vegetable garden subsequently make oxygen for a Kombucha tea brewery, which in return provides carbon dioxide for the plants. With the installation of an anaerobic digester to produce biogas from agricultural waste, The Plant hopes to be producing all of its own energy by the time it is fully renovated and completely operational in 2016.[18]

In Manchester in the United Kingdom, a similar initiative called the Alpha Farm is at an earlier stage of development. Here the plan is to develop a five-year vertical farm project as part of the Manchester International Festival in 2013.[19] Input has been obtained from Dickson Despommier, although sadly initial plans to convert an existing tower block have had to be abandoned as unfeasible. Nevertheless, the Alpha Farm's proponents are still hopeful that they will be successful in bringing some form of indoor urban agriculture to the city. Even if this is not in the form of a vertical farm, here as in many other locations the interest generated by potential high-rise agriculture may serve as a useful springboard for more down-to-earth forms of urban food production.

Most cities will probably always rely on at least some food being shipped in from a remote location. Nevertheless, as we try to fix the world, the idea of growing at least a little food in every urban location will probably need to be embraced. Before many vertical farms rise to meet the food require-ments of an entire neighbourhood, an increasing number of urban back gardens, allotments, conservatories and roof gardens are therefore likely to be put to good use to help shift more food production into the city.

Even city dwellers without gardens may start to grow a little of their own produce. To this end, just one initiative encouraging local food production on a microscale is the Windowfarms Project. This has the goal of empowering urban dwellers to grow some of their own food indoors in all seasons, with the members of its online community collaboratively innovating toward 'more sustainable cities and an improved urban quality of life'.[20]

The Windowfarms Project is based around the concept of 'crowdsourcing' (as I discuss in depth in chapter 5) and R&D-I-Y (research and develop it yourself). Crops are grown organically in vertical, hydroponic growing systems in which a pump circulates a 'liquid circuit' that provides water and nutrients to the roots of stacked plants. Window-farm units can be positioned in almost any window, and purchased in a variety of kits from windowfarms.org. Alternatively, many Windowfarmers self-build from online designs, with their homemade hydroponic systems constructed in part from old plastic bottles and other recycled materials. Already there are over 36,000 Windowfarmers harvesting a salad or two from an average-sized window at least once a week.

Some architects are now trying to capture and implement the ethos of community projects like Windowfarms on a far grander scale. To this end, agriculture is being integrated into new-build urban environments called 'smartcities'. In these developments, a key focus is on building entire cities that can meet all of their citizens' needs. While one of the most basic human needs is a constant food supply, for centuries this requirement has been ignored by architects and town planners who have taken for granted that organic nourishment will be transported in from elsewhere. In sharp contrast, and as argued by renowned 'eco-warrior' architect C.J. Lim, a central component of any smartcity is urban agriculture and the establishment of an ecological symbiosis between nature, society and the built form.[21]

Just one example of a smartcity is a new town centre being created for the 200,000 residents of Guangming in Shenzhen,

China. As the country industrializes, already more than half of China's population has moved from the countryside to urban areas, in turn putting intense pressure on systems for food supply. Recognizing this, the Guangming New Town Smartcity is a new kind of hybrid urban area directly surrounded by arable land. On this land traditional dairy, vegetable and fruit farming is being retained and modernized with hydroponics and other advanced agricultural techniques. Pigeon and cow sheds, floral gardens and arable laboratories are also being built into the very heart of the city. Grazing and arable land is additionally located on the vast roof spaces of huge, circular towers, with city-centre growing spaces for cultivating vegetables provided by eighty vertical farms.

The Guangming development allows city dwellers who were previously farmers to grow food part-time while also undertaking traditional city occupations. In time, the Guangming Smartcity is intended to become a model for more sustainable, local living as China industrializes further. Or as its architect explains:

> The existing farming community . . . will play an important role in sustaining a skilled workforce in the local area that are able to run farms as viable businesses. Local food production will establish a strong sense of community and sustainably help reduce energy and fuel consumption from food transportation. Guangming Smartcity locates people where the food grows instead of moving food to the people.[22]

MORE LOCAL MANUFACTURE

In addition to embracing some level of urban agriculture, as transportation costs skyrocket we will increasingly need to start manufacturing a great many things far closer to home.

There are in essence also two ways to achieve this. The first is to employ traditional technologies that will permit many nations and regions to return to the local manufacture of those items that they have currently chosen to outsource to other nations. The second is to employ new technologies that will allow the local manufacture of products that until this point in time have proved impossible or entirely uneconomic to make on a local scale.

Over the past few decades a great deal of 'low-value' traditional manufacturing has migrated from the United States and Western Europe to many rapidly developing nations, and not least China. This has, however, only been possible due to an abundant supply of relatively cheap oil. As petroleum becomes scarcer and more expensive, and as labour costs rise in the developing world, the production of many essential and relatively essential 'low value' goods – including clothing, crockery, cutlery, medical items and kitchen appliances – will therefore have to recommence in Europe and the United States. The required knowledge to achieve this already exists. The question is simply how soon and how readily the populations of these regions will accept this new, post-petroleum reality.

Even more fundamental than the return of basic manufacturing to many 'developed' nations will be a new era of micro manufacturing on a very local level. Several cutting-edge technologies will soon allow any scale of business to manufacture items that previously had to be made in a large factory that was inevitably remote from the majority of its customers. Not least, 3D printing and synthetic biology look set to empower a new wave of localization.

3D printing does what it says on the tin. Whereas a traditional 2D printer is limited to making marks on paper, a 3D printer uses an 'additive manufacturing' process to output three-dimensional objects one very thin layer at a time. Already a range of 3D printing technologies are in commercial application, with one of the most common being fused deposition modelling (FDM). Here objects are created via the controlled output of a heated thermoplastic from a print head nozzle.

Other current 3D printing methods build objects by laying down a great many layers of powder. The granules of the build material are fused together by a process known as selective laser sintering (SLS) or selective laser melting (SLM), or else glued into solid forms by selectively spraying on a binder solution. While FDM can only create plastic objects, powder technologies can already 3D print in a wide range of materials. These include glass, ceramics, steel, titanium, aluminium, bronze, sterling silver and gold.

3D printers capable of manufacturing end-use plastic components can now be purchased for just over $1,000, although most commercial machines currently cost $10,000+. Prices are, however, dropping rapidly. As we shall see in chapter 5, there are also some thriving online communities whose members are developing open source 3D printers that can be built by enthusiasts for a few hundred dollars. Local, customized manufacturing is therefore already becoming a distinct possibility.

3D printers will also increasingly allow at least some industrial processes to be 'dematerialized'. Rather than trading globally in physical goods, companies will instead be able to sell their 3D designs for local printout, hence reducing those resources currently consumed in transportation. Spare parts will also be able to be stored digitally rather than physically, only to be printed out when and where required. In turn, this should make almost any spare part constantly available, so allowing many items to be repaired rather than discarded when they are broken. The profound implications of 3D printing to enable resource savings via dematerialization and design for repair are discussed in more depth in chapters 3 and 4.

While 3D printing is poised to allow the local manufacture of complex, custom products and components, synthetic biology will soon permit an increasing variety of valuable commodities to be organically grown. The idea behind synthetic biology is to apply an engineering mentality to genetic modification, and in the process to permit the creation of radically transformed or entirely artificial living things. While conventional genetic engineering typically splices just one or a few new genes into an existing plant or animal, synthetic biology rearranges the components of life in dramatically new ways for productive purposes.

Synthetic biologists have already started to build up catalogues of standardized 'Biobrick' components that may be plugged together like Lego to build new forms of designer life. This very new engineering practice was first brought to public attention in May 2010 when the J. Craig Venter Institute (JCVI) in California created the first entirely synthetic life form. Christened 'JCVI-syn1.0', this self-replicating, single-celled organism was based on an existing *Mycoplasma capricolum* bacterium. Yet at its core was an entirely synthetic, 1.08 million base pair genome spliced together in the JCVI laboratory. To prove the point, the JCVI scientists even encoded an e-mail address into their creation's artificial DNA.

Over the next few decades synthetic biology has the potential to kick-start a new age in which many essential raw materials will be able to be sourced locally. For example, a team from the Korea Advanced Institute of Science & Technology have already managed to build an *E. coli* bacterium that can transform corn or sugar cane directly into a bioplastic known as polylactic acid (PLA). While the production of PLA is possible using conventional technologies, a complex chemical post-processing is required. In contrast, once synthetic biologists have done their stuff, the potential will exist for PLA to be manufactured directly by synthetic bacteria fed with simple organic foodstuffs. Already most FDM 3D printers can make objects from PLA. In principle, it may therefore become possible for local manufacturers to grow raw materials for 3D printing in large vats in their back yards.

Another synthetic biology pioneer is OPX Biotechnologies. Here a new micro-organism is being created that can manufacture a bioacrylic from corn, sugar cane, or any other form of cellulose.[23]

Petroleum-based acrylics are an essential raw material used in the manufacture of paints, adhesives and detergents. The application of synthetic biology to permit the creation of bioacrylics will therefore be a very welcome development as it will reduce our reliance on dwindling petroleum supplies. Further, it will potentially allow acrylics to be produced in any location capable of sustaining traditional agriculture or running a vertical farm.

Synthetic biology additionally holds much promise for the manufacture of biofuels. Indeed, following the creation of the first synthetic bacteria by JCVI, one of its sister companies – Synthetic Genomics – filed several patents in this area. Already a Californian company called LS9 is developing a synthetic *E. coli* bacterium that is able to ferment two forms of biodiesel from agricultural waste. Meanwhile, several research teams are focused on producing third generation bioethanol from waste products – including animal and human faeces – rather than from crops such as corn or sugar cane.

Synthetic biology developments will soon also allow biofuels to be manufactured from algae. Appropriate algae will be able to be cultivated in hanging gardens or pods in virtually any location. In time this will enable the local production of some petroleum substitutes from air, water and sunlight using photosynthesis. Already Austrian pioneer

Ecodura has created a commercial photo bioreactor that can efficiently mass produce algae, and which could in the future be used to organically manufacture biofuels and bioplastics.

Unfortunately, due to the relatively high resource intensity of biofuel production, biofuels will never be able to replace more than a relatively small fraction of our current petroleum usage. So please, do not conclude here that synthetic biology can provide a complete solution to the challenge of Peak Oil, as sadly it cannot. Even so, the application of synthetic biology will allow us to locally produce those reduced quantities of liquid fuels that we will continue to require in the decades and even centuries ahead.

Today, while synthetic biology is focused on the creation of artificial micro-organisms, in the future it could potentially be used to engineer synthetic plants or even synthetic animals. After all, if a synthetic bacterium can be created capable of transforming organic matter into a biofuel or bioplastic, then in theory a plant could be engineered from which biofuels or bioplastics could be directly harvested. Nature, after all, already indicates the potential, with rubber plants having for centuries been harvested for their latex.

Today, the banana is the only food that is grown in its own protective wrapper. But with a little synthetic biology applied, in the future a great many pre-packaged foods could potentially be grown on new synthetic species of trees. This would not only save a great deal of packaging, but would remove the requirement for packaging (or packaging raw materials) to be imported by local food producers.

The near-future development of both 3D printing and synthetic biology offers an enormous potential to migrate the production of many products and raw materials to the local scale. Since the beginning of the Industrial Revolution, we have come to rely on increasingly complex and dedicated production technologies that have had to be centralized far away from most consumers. The promise of both 3D printing and synthetic biology is that complex, multi-purpose production technologies may soon be applied at a very local level. A 3D printer may potentially never make the same product or component twice, so allowing local businesses to become highly effective Jacks and Jills of all trades. A few decades hence, broad-market local businesses with 3D printing facilities may therefore be able to meet a wide range of local customer requirements just as traditional craftspeople always did in the pre-industrial age.

Perhaps even more startlingly, the promise and beauty of synthetic biology is that it may increasingly allow the highly complex production technology of life itself to be harnessed for a very wide range of purposes in almost any location. Both farmers and industrial producers will simply obtain the synthetic micro-organisms or plants they need from a biotech lab. They will then cultivate, breed and feed them to organically produce whatever their local customers require.

Reducing the Daily Commute

A great many natural resources – and in particular large quantities of petroleum – are currently used to move human beings around at either end of the working day. Inevitably as fossil fuels become scarcer and more expensive, this mass ritual will have to be curtailed. Indeed, many people will simply not be able to earn enough to afford to travel a long distance to their place of work. Given that severe logistical limits on where most people could work existed until the middle of the last century, this should also come as no great surprise. Long-distance commutes really are an unsustainable aberration of the modern age.

In the relatively near future, it is likely that many people will need to obtain a new job nearer to where they live, or else relocate closer to their workplace. Given that Peak Oil could well be with us by 2020, this is a harsh near-future reality that far more people need to start to very actively consider. As we shall see in the next chapter, alternative energy solutions are extremely unlikely to make energy and transportation less expensive. A great many people are therefore going to have to start making unfamiliar trade-offs to ensure that they can get to work and so maintain their employment.

Others may be able to work from home, perhaps engaging in new urban agricultural or craft activities that will be in increased demand as local communities de-globalize. For some, teleworking will also be an option. This is where work is performed for a geographically distant organization using a computer and the Internet. Teleworking therefore has the potential to transform many types of office-based employment.

Back in the early 1980s, Rank Xerox conducted experiments that demonstrated teleworking's technological if not social feasibility.[24] Since that time, the practice has become fairly widespread, with many academic and industry studies having analyzed its advantages and drawbacks. On the positive side, it has generally been reported that teleworkers are more productive than office based workers, can achieve an improved work-life balance, and fairly obviously spend less time travelling. Most organizations also benefit from real estate and other cost savings when they set up a teleworking initiative, as well as experiencing reduced staff turnover. On the other hand, teleworkers often feel isolated from their colleagues and unable to ever escape their job. Some organizations have also reported that managing teleworkers can prove problematic. In particular, it can sometimes prove difficult to integrate groups of teleworkers into effective teams.

At present the jury remains out regarding whether teleworking has more benefits or drawbacks for both employees and organizations. This is, however, before the long-term benefits in terms of resource savings are considered. When they are, almost any teleworking initiative becomes incredibly attractive, as capital and transportation resources are saved and greenhouse gas emissions cut.

People and organizations who learn how to make teleworking successful today will clearly be far better prepared for a Peak Oil world in which many will simply not have the option of an extended daily commute. Those who work with their hands to physically make things or deliver services such as cleaning, product maintenance or healthcare will probably always have to travel at least some distance to their place of employment (or else get others to travel to them). In contrast, those who largely work with their minds in offices will fairly soon find it hard to justify or afford a daily migration beyond the distance they can walk or cycle.

* * *

EMBRACING LOCALIZATION

For three decades the mantra in business has been globalization, with companies large and small encouraged to set foot on the global stage. In contrast, many of the smart and successful businesses of the 2020s and beyond are likely to be those that work out how to meet the most critical, immediate needs of the people who live fairly close to them. This means that the goal of many companies will become that of establishing local product ecosystems that allow them to meet local consumer needs by providing them with products produced from locally-sourced raw materials wherever possible.

If we are to fix the world – let alone to maintain industrial civilization – localization has to become the new globalization. For individuals as well as organizations, this will also involve a great many changes. For a start, where and how most people shop will be transformed. Over the past few decades, the trend to buy things in very large, out-of-town supermarkets and hypermarkets has diverted the distribution of food and other goods entirely in the wrong direction. Some large supermarket chains may reap resource savings via sophisticated logistics integration. This said, as and when rising oil prices make it impossible for many people to run a powered vehicle, so local stores will again start to flourish as the majority of the population return to foraging for supplies on their local high street.

The tourism and leisure sectors are additionally set to be radically transformed by a pending wave of localization. Less than 50 years ago most people never went near an aircraft, and yet still managed to live perfectly happy lives. As the barrel of oil consumed by the average international traveller ceases to be both readily affordable and available, so casually hopping on a plane for a brief jaunt overseas will soon become no more than a distant memory of an unsustainable past.

This is not to say that in the 2020s and beyond nobody will fly. But air travel will be far less common and only undertaken out of real necessity or on very special occasions. In recent years the word 'staycation' has entered the common lexicon to describe a vacation taken either at home or in a local region. Just as the package tour and cheap air travel were the tourism innovations of the 1980s and 1990s, so the staycation looks set to become the mainstream tourism development of the next few decades.

Having read this chapter you could be forgiven for believing that I am predicting and promoting a return to a bygone age. To the extent that in the fairly near future most people will have to source far more things locally this is absolutely the case. However, even though in the future we will have to physically live more locally, we will do so on a planet that will continue to possess the extraordinary global communications platform of the Internet. While for the majority of recorded history, human beings lived locally in settlements, towns and even cities that were regionally and globally isolated, this will subsequently not be the case in the more local world of tomorrow. No longer will so many of us be able to hop on a plane at a whim. But the vast majority will still be able to communicate and share near-instantaneously as global citizens.

What all of the above implies is that in the coming decades we will localize a great deal of our low-value material production and trade, while continuing to globalize our production and exchange of higher-value items and dematerialized digital media. As we shall explore further in chapter 3, the existence of technologies such as cloud computing and 3D printing will increasingly facilitate this transition in a world that learns to transport information more, and people and things somewhat less.

Like it or not, localization is soon set to eclipse traditional globalization for the simple reason that today's trade-anywhere global economy has been built on the assumed foundation of endless fossil fuel supply. Unfortunately, that bedrock treasure of hundreds of millions of years of collected photosynthesis is starting to be seriously depleted. Inevitably, we will therefore soon have no choice but to change our ways. Just one consequence will have to be more local living. But fairly obviously there will be many other implications. Not least, as we shall explore in the next chapter, our future lifestyles will also have to be far more energy efficient than those we lead today.

2

LOW ENERGY LIFESTYLES

In June every year BP publishes its *Statistical Review of World Energy*. This annual report contains a pretty comprehensive overview of global energy production and reserves, and provides the best barometer of human energy use on this planet.

Despite the ongoing crisis in the global economy, the *2011 Review* revealed a growth in global energy usage in 2010 of 5.6 per cent.[25] This was the highest annual rate of increase since 1973. The *2011 Review* also indicated that in 2010 energy consumption grew more rapidly than economic activity, so in turn signalling the ever-increasing energy intensity of industrial civilization.

A year later, the *2012 Review* thankfully showed that the annual increase in global energy consumption had slowed to 2.5 per cent. This was generally explained by the impact of the 'Arab Spring' in early 2011, coupled with the earthquake and tsunami that devastated Japan in March, and which had immediate implications for both power generation and energy demand.[26]

Despite the involved human tragedy, it has to be a good thing that energy consumption grew less steeply in 2011 than it did in 2010. This said, it does appear that, whatever happens, human energy use only continues to increase. The problem is that the Petroleum Age has bred a culture of unlimited energy rights and unconstrained energy expectations. Even in the face of climate change and Peak Oil, it will therefore take significant efforts to persuade collective humanity to use less power.

Investments in 'alternative' forms of energy are thankfully now growing rapidly. Yet switching to fossil fuel substitutes can at best constitute only half of any sustainable energy solution. In the same way that we will have to adjust to living more locally, so over the next few decades we also need to embrace modes of living that are far less energy intensive.

ENERGY OUT & ENERGY IN

Many reporters in the mainstream media continue to deny the looming impact of climate change and Peak Oil. To me this head-in-the-sand attitude toward all of our tomorrows is very worrying. Yet just as alarming is the way in which many other mainstream media sources seem intent on convincing us that a transition to wind, wave and solar energy will sort everything out and allow us to go on living just as we do today.

I happen to be a great fan of wind, wave and solar power. It is indeed excellent that about 3 per cent and rising of world energy comes from the wind; that commercial wave farms are now coming online; and that solar power generation capacity has increased nearly ten-fold over the past five years. The US Department of Energy's SunShot Initiative is even hoping to make solar energy cost competitive with fossil fuels by the end of the decade.[27]

In 2011 alone, 41 gigawatts of new wind turbine capacity and 28.4 gigawatts of new photovoltaic solar power installations were added to the global electricity generation infrastructure. These installations equated to increases of 25 per cent and 73 per cent respectively.[28] The alternative energy sector is therefore certainly on a roll. However – and it is a really big however – we must not make the mistake of believing that 'renewable' energy sources can serve as a replacement for even a reasonable proportion of current fossil fuel usage. Nor should we fool ourselves into thinking that 'renewable' energy sources are actually 'renewable' at all.

The simple fact which so many continue to ignore is that every means of *producing energy* also requires the *consumption* of energy and physical resources. For example, to obtain energy from fossil fuels we need to conduct exploration, build machinery, extract the fuel, transport it, refine it, build power plants to burn it, decommission those plants at the end of their useful life, and so on. Alternative energy sources similarly demand quite significant energy and resource investments. For example, wind and wave power require turbines and related infrastructure to be built and maintained to enable the production of electricity. And we are not just talking about electrical systems here. To many people's surprise, the construction of a 20 megawatt wind farm can consume over 10,000 tonnes of concrete.[29]

Solar power plants similarly require the production of photovoltaic solar panels, or else mirrors, piping systems and turbines if they are based around concentrated solar power technologies that convert heat rather than light into electricity. It should really come as no surprise that none of this infrastructure can be produced without using energy and raw materials, and that no mechanism for generating 'renewable' energy will last forever. Any sensible assessment of any energy source – alternative or otherwise – therefore has to be mindful of its net energy contribution. This is a measure of the energy obtained from an energy source after accounting for the energy consumed in its production.

Most commonly, those who analyze net energy work with a measure known as EROI, or the 'energy return on investment'. This is a ratio of energy output to energy input. So, for example, if the production of five units of energy requires the consumption of one unit of energy, the EROI of the involved energy source is 5:1.

THE NET ENERGY TIME BOMB

The easiest forms of petroleum to extract from the ground freely gush from a well and do not need to be pumped or otherwise forced to the surface. Back in the 1930s, some of these 'sweetest' petroleum sources had an EROI of around 100:1.[30] This meant that, for every unit of energy consumed in obtaining them, a quite staggering 100 units of energy were produced when the oil was burnt to power cars or other machinery.

Today, very-easy-to-extract crude oil is rare, with conventional petroleum having a global EROI of no more than 40:1. The net energy obtained from petroleum will also diminish further as crude oil gets harder to find and extract. For example, pumping oil from a very deep well out at sea is a more energy-intensive proposition that extracting it from a freely gushing onshore field, and hence will result in a lower net energy yield.

Those in denial about Peak Oil often pin their hopes on the mass exploitation of unconventional oil, such as that starting to be obtained from shale or oil sands. Unfortunately, in addition to releasing more greenhouse gasses than burning petroleum, unconventional oils also have a lower EROI ratio. For example, the EROI for shale oil is typically about 5:1,[31] while for oil extracted from oil sands the EROI is usually between 5:1 and 7:1.[32]

The net energy yields of biofuels are also sadly far lower than those of petroleum. Indeed, some early biofuels actually required more energy resources to be invested to produce them than they could finally yield. Today, this situation is improved, although the EROI of most biofuels is typically no more than 3:1 and unlikely to rise further.[33] As I noted in the last chapter, the development of next generation biofuels – while important – therefore cannot provide a solution to Peak Oil and our future energy requirements.

When it comes to other energy sources, cited EROI ratios for coal vary between about 20:1 and 80:1, while hydroelectric power is generally agreed to deliver an EROI of somewhere between 20:1 and 40:1. Natural gas has an EROI of about 10:1, with a similar ratio usually calculated for nuclear power.[34] Wind power can deliver an EROI of up to 18:1 (although frequently far less), while photovoltaic solar cells deliver a maximum EROI of about 7:1. EROI ratios for concentrated solar power are far lower, with a reliable EROI for wave power yet to be established.

It should be noted that net energy ratios are extremely difficult to calculate, and hence that the figures I have just cited are hotly contended. This important point noted, no serious analyst disputes that the net energy of petroleum continues to fall. Nor is there any disagreement that the net energy obtained from all major alternative energy sources is far lower than that of conventional fossil fuels. What the previous few paragraphs therefore tell us is that, while wind, wave, solar and even nuclear energy may be able to fuel the world of tomorrow, they will not be able to power a clone of today. Nor will non-conventional fossil fuels or biofuels be able to deliver current levels of power generation, as their EROI ratio is also relatively low. For a while we could produce electricity from coal. But conventional coal power stations are major emitters of greenhouse gases, while clean coal-burning technologies deliver an EROI as low as 5:1.[35]

A few decades hence, to go on consuming energy in the manner that we do today would require not just a substantial switch to alternative energy sources, but an increase in the scale of the global energy sector by a factor of maybe five or more. Given that about 10 per cent of the world's gross domestic product is already spent on energy,[36] this kind of order-of-magnitude increase in the size of the global energy industry is simply not possible. (But, I hear some of you cry, what if we just had a far larger global economy? Well, unfortunately that would not help given that the energy intensity of global economic activity is currently increasing).

The net energy time bomb is now well and truly ticking, with the net energy output of any known, widely available future energy source being lower than that of the conventional petroleum on which we have built our civilization.[37] This means that, even if we foolishly ignored climate change and fully exploited all forms of unconventional fossil fuels, the total annual net energy available to global civilization will still soon fall because of the increasing fraction of available energy consumed in energy production.[38]

Due to the net energy time bomb, whatever happens in the next few decades we will have to transition to more energy efficient lifestyles. Even if half of the companies on the planet became alternative energy providers, there is simply no physical or economic mechanism that could continue to deliver the quantity of power that the world consumes today.

ENERGY AWARENESS & RESPONSIBILITY

In a perfect world our collective response to the net energy time bomb would be an immediate reduction in many personal and industrial energy-consuming activities, coupled with a rapid transition to lower-power devices. But we do not live in a perfect world, and hence our journey to a less energy-intensive form of civilization is going to be long, twisted, and probably very uncomfortable indeed. People and organizations will need convincing of the need to change, and then educating about how to live and operate in a different manner. And all this is destined to take rather a lot of time that we really do not have.

One of the first and most important ways for an individual to start developing a low energy lifestyle – or for a business to reduce its energy consumption – is to increase their energy awareness and associated sense of energy responsibility. This is also far harder than most people realize, and requires a fundamental change of mindset so that energy consumption is consciously factored into almost every decision made. Practically every choice enacted in an industrialized society – from what food we eat and how we cook it, to where we travel and how we get there – has an implication for our energy usage. And increasing our energy awareness and responsibility is about becoming as conscious of this as possible.

To try and increase energy awareness, many governments and energy companies are intent on the roll-out of smart meters. These have a digital display that shows the energy use of a home or business in real-time. Once a smart meter has been fitted, people will in theory gain a greater knowledge of the amount of electricity used by each device they turn on. So the argument goes, they will then realize the quantity of power they are wasting, and will be more likely to turn off devices that do not need to be draining power.

To some extent the roll-out of smart meters is an excellent idea. But it also needs to be accepted that installing smart meters does not directly decrease the amount of power that we do or may use. Indeed, as powered devices, smart meters actually increase our energy consumption, if by a very small amount. Far more fundamentally, I would also argue that nobody should need a smart meter to tell them that their energy consumption will go down if they switch off lights, chargers, computers and televisions when they are not in use. Fitting a smart meter may instantly make a person or business feel good and even *believe* that they are actually doing something positive for the planet. But it is actually turning devices down or off that really matters. Excessive measurement is not the answer. And there is just no getting away from this fact.

OK, so I may be a cynic. Even so, if somebody believes that a fire, oven, charger, dishwasher or 60 inch plasma TV really needs to be turned on, then they are not going to turn it off when a smart meter tells them how much power it is using. And if they do not think something needs to be turned on, they will not have needed a smart meter to tell them that either.

At the end of the day, while increasing energy awareness is a very positive first step, it will only lead to more energy-efficient lifestyles if coupled with radically altered attitudes toward energy responsibility. It may be that smart meters will make some people and companies aware of the money they are wasting, and that this in turn will lead them to reduce their energy use. But true energy awareness really needs to mentally link every decision we make to an internal appreciation of our energy responsibility. When we turn on any powered device today we inevitably deprive somebody tomorrow of being able to consume energy in some form. Living with this understanding ought not to handicap our entire existence. But it should make us think about our wider responsibilities as timeshare occupiers of this planet.

As parents commonly bemoan, most children have no appreciation of the value of money. In the same way, today most adults in the industrialized world have little or no appreciation of the true value of energy. And that is the key thing we somehow must change. Using energy is a privilege, not a right, and one that needs to become more widely associated with a long-term sense of responsibility.

Low Power Devices

Once people or businesses have increased their level of energy awareness and responsibility, they can basically do two things. The first is to live their lives or run their businesses differently, while the second is to continue to do many of the same things, but using devices that consume less power. The first of these options is likely to involve measures such as turning on electrical devices only when deemed absolutely necessary, making fewer powered journeys, and adopting a more local lifestyle that reduces the need to travel and to transport objects over long distances. We all know that we can use less energy if we simply do less powered stuff. Whether people and companies choose to do this or not is basically a question of individuals and managers deciding to take some personal responsibility for the world of tomorrow.

When it comes to the second option of using lower power devices, many people and organizations could be assisted with the provision of far better information. Many larger electrical goods – such as washing machines and refrigerators – are now commonly labelled with their energy usage and relative energy efficiency. Most people who drive are also very conscious of the fuel usage of their vehicle per litre or gallon. Even so, far more could be done to raise awareness of potential power savings.

Right now I am sitting at a desktop PC and consuming electricity. This said, I am also trying to exercise some level of energy responsibility, as the computer on which I am typing these words is based around Intel's low-power Atom processor. The 19-inch monitor I am looking at is also a low-power model from NEC. This means that, in total, I am consuming 41 watts of power each hour (20 watts for the PC and 21 watts for the monitor). This is not insignificant. But it is far less than the 200 watts of electricity that my previous desktop PC and monitor were using per hour only a few years ago.

Most people and businesses are unaware of the opportunity to switch to low-power computer technology that could cut their energy usage by up to 80 per cent. This is amazing given that the average desktop PC already costs more in energy bills in its lifetime than it does to purchase in the first place. It is therefore bizarre that, in most stores, computers are not even labelled with their power usage. Nor are low-power devices commonly on sale.

As in so many other areas, the problem is not the technical creation of low power devices, but convincing people that they want them (or convincing companies that their customers will want them). In computing in particular, so many good solutions already exist. For example, I recently came across an award-winning, multi-seat PC software platform called Ecoware that allows one standard desktop PC to be shared by six users.[39] For all basic office computing tasks, no functionality is lost, but energy use is drastically reduced. But are most large offices and call centres adopting such technology? No, we all know that they are not. Such systems are even less common than low power individual PCs. And the problem really is one of achieving attitude shift.

As you may know if you are reading this book, I run two YouTube channels called ExplainingTheFuture and ExplainingComputers. A few years ago, I uploaded a video to the latter in which I showed how I built the low power Atom PC on which I am currently working. I am not here suggesting that everybody can or should build their own low power PC. Rather, I mention this video because it has attracted over 150,000 views and more than 1,000 comments. Some of those who have left a comment have asked technical or practical questions about the build or its components. But by far the majority have said something to the effect that they would not want a low energy PC. Indeed, comments like 'My PC uses 1500 watts', 'just my fans use more power', and 'why would someone **want** a computer like this?' are representative of most of the feedback.

Sadly we live in a world in which owning higher power rather than lower power devices is still often viewed as a good thing. Male egos in particular are frequently boosted via the ownership of pimped-up, highest-power-possible hardware ranging from gaming PCs to automobiles. A desire to consume energy regardless of the future consequences is now deeply culturally embedded in many parts of the world. It is for this reason that the European Union and other bodies have felt the need to legislate to force a transition to lower power devices from televisions to light bulbs. Though legislation can only go so far.

In less than a decade we could all be using lower power computers, next-generation LED light bulbs, and all manner of less energy-intensive technology. At present the two drivers toward such use are legislative imposition and a desire to save money by reducing energy costs. These drivers may be both welcome and in many instances powerful. Nevertheless, to really fix the world the driver somehow needs to become an inherent desire by most people to want to use less energy.

Today, those pioneers who embrace low power devices usually need to spend a great deal of time seeking out new technologies that buck the trend. To join them, more people need to start asking questions like 'what is the energy consumption of the device I currently use?' and 'do devices exist that use less energy to accomplish roughly the same thing?' If research reveals the answer to the second question is 'yes', then a decision needs to be made regarding when and if switching to a new device can be afforded and will result in net energy savings. The more people who become pioneers and start asking such questions the better. Not least this is because, once enough people have trailblazed as pioneers, low power devices will finally enter the mainstream. If we are lucky, advertisers and marketeers may even start to take notice.

GOING OFF GRID

In the early 1970s, and in the wake of the publication of *The Limits to Growth*,[40] an important minority started to take a practical interest in more sustainable living. At the time, a key means of achieving this was believed to be going 'off-grid' to generate one's own power. Few early pioneers managed to make this work completely and to become entirely self-sufficient. People's interest therefore soon waned. But several decades on, off-grid power generation is once again attracting a great deal of attention.

As already discussed, every means of generating an artificial energy supply will consume resources, and hence putting up your own wind turbine or solar panel does not necessarily constitute a magical means of generating power in a more efficient manner. Indeed, the net energy output of most off-grid power generation hardware is likely to be lower than that of larger-scale, on-grid power plants. On the upside, off-grid power can often be matched closely with actual energy requirements, and also suffers no energy loss in long-distance transmission.

Several straightforward means of off-grid power generation are now readily available. These include solar thermal energy systems, ground source heat pumps, anaerobic digesters, wind turbines, photovoltaic solar cells, and various forms of kinetic power generation. Of these, the first two are usually the most net energy-efficient, as they use simple technologies to make a direct use of heat from the environment.

Solar thermal energy (STE) systems are a tried and tested technology for heating domestic hot water and central heating radiators. Systems consist of rooftop solar collection panels that contain pipes under glass through which a liquid is pumped. The liquid circulates in a closed loop to transfer heat from the Sun to a hot water tank. Some top-up heat from a gas or electric system is almost always required. Even so, even in the United Kingdom, British Gas estimates that STE systems could supply 60 per cent of the energy necessary to heat hot water in most homes.[41]

Ground source heat pumps use buried pipes to extract heat from the ground. One or a few pipes are sunk tens of metres down a vertical borehole, or if enough land is available a large loop of pipes is buried not that far from the surface. In either design, a liquid circulates through the pipework to carry heat to an exchanger where it is captured via a heat pump and used to warm water in a boiler. Electricity is required to run the heat pump. But as with an STE system, the use of ground source piping can significantly reduce the requirement to draw on grid power.[42]

Anaerobic digesters use bacteria to convert plant and animal waste into a biogas that mainly consists of methane and carbon dioxide. This can then be burnt to produce heat or electricity. Alternatively, if the carbon dioxide and other contaminant gases are removed, the resultant biomethane can be injected into the mains gas supply or used to power vehicles. The waste from an anaerobic digester can additionally be used as a fertilizer.[43]

Off-grid wind turbines – otherwise known as 'small wind systems' – typically produce a few kilowatts of low-voltage power. A transformer and inverter can be used to allow this energy to help power traditional household or office devices. Alternatively, small wind systems may be used to charge batteries and to run low-voltage devices such as laptops or music systems. Low-voltage immersion heaters also allow wind turbines to heat hot water, and can allow excess energy to be 'dumped' into hot water tanks rather than wasted when battery packs are fully charged. As very low power LED bulbs become the norm over the next decade, many households could power all of their lighting from a small rooftop turbine that charges a set of batteries whenever the wind is blowing.

While wind turbines do have a reputation for being both ugly and noisy, more aesthetic and quieter models are now arriving on the market. For example, QuietRevolution sells a very-low-noise, vertical-axis wind turbine that resembles a spinning DNA molecule. Mounted on a 9-metre tower, the system can produce about 7 kilowatts in a good wind location.

In recent years photovoltaic (PV) solar panels have begun to adorn many a domestic rooftop to generate a little off-grid power from the Sun's rays. Typical domestic PV installations produce a few kilowatts of power, and like small wind turbines may either be connected to a transformer and inverter to help power traditional devices, or can run low power hardware via a battery storage system. Across the United Kingdom, many PV installations have been prompted by generous government feed-in tariffs that allow homeowners to sell surplus power back to the grid. At the other end of the spectrum, as PV technologies improve it is quite likely that some future devices will generate a little of their own power from small, integrated solar panels. For example, some future laptop computers are likely to have a solar panel incorporated into their lid.

Finally, electricity may be generated off-grid from anything that naturally moves. For example, clockwork radios and lighting systems are available that store and release the energy that a human being winds into a spring. Low-power clockwork laptops have even been trialled in parts of Africa. Plans are also afoot for personal power systems that compress piezoelectric crystals to generate electricity.

For example, researchers at the Georgia Institute of Technology have experimented with piezoelectric textile fibres that could be woven into clothing. These would generate a little power each time they rubbed against each other.[44] In the future, the movement of your jacket or trousers may therefore be able to power your MP3 player or mobile phone. In fact, as the net energy available to humanity continues to fall, it is likely that more and more devices will include an option to at least partially power themselves from human motion. We may even see off-grid power systems that harness domestic animal power to generate small quantities of electricity.

All of the aforementioned forms of off-grid power generation have their benefits and drawbacks. None in isolation will help to fix the world, and indeed many may result in less efficient net energy production than on-grid power plants. Even so, the widespread use of off-grid power is likely to prove critical in our transition to low energy lifestyles. Not least this is because the people who generate even a little of their own electricity will become those who most appreciate the natural resources and human labour inherent in power generation. In turn, those people who generate off-grid power will seek to use electricity as efficiently as possible. After all, wasting energy produced far away in a power plant is one thing. But wasting energy that you produce locally yourself is quite another, as the challenges and limits of supply will be far more immediate and obvious.

MAKING THE TRANSITION

In his lovely if worrying book *The Long Descent*, John Michael Greer paints a picture of the slow decline of industrial civilization in the face of falling net energy yields. As he argues, 'during the last two centuries, the quickest way to prosper was to ride the wave of progress, using more energy, more resources, and more technology than your competitors. For the next two centuries, the quickest way to prosper will stand this rule on its head'.[45]

In his above contention Greer is almost certainly correct. In respect of both more local living and low energy lifestyles – as well as several of the other developments detailed in this book – the route to future happiness and prosperity is likely to involve consuming things and energy less, while valuing things and energy more. In such pursuit, an increasing number of individuals and companies will probably start to generate at least a little off-grid power. Today, many continue to dismiss rooftop wind turbines or solar water heating systems on the basis that they 'will not produce enough power to be worth the effort'. But only a decade or two out this will no longer be the case.

Technologies for off-grid power generation are likely to improve, if not dramatically. But what will critically happen is that grid energy will become so much scarcer and more expensive that every little bit of power from whatever source will increasingly matter. Not long from now, energy will simply no longer be able to be dismissed as 'somebody else's problem'. Instead, more and more of us will come to appreciate energy production as a broad on- and off-grid collage to which everybody will need to contribute at some level.

Off-grid power is almost certain to become very common as lower energy lifestyles take hold. In turn this will mean that the buried heat pipe in the garden or the solar panel on the roof are able to contribute a greater and greater proportion of a family or company's individual energy requirement. Or as Greer so nicely puts it:

If the last three hundred years funnelled wealth to those who exploited fossil fuels to the fullest, and allowed them to build centralized, technologically driven economic structures, then the next three hundred years will see exactly the opposite. Success will go to those who get ahead of depletion curves by reducing their reliance on fossil fuels further than others, and by relying instead on human skills and sustainable, low-intensity energy inputs.[46]

Already some people are making practical preparations to transition to a lower energy, lower carbon world. For example, there are now about 1,000 local, regional or national 'Transition Initiatives' across 35 countries. Together these form part of the growing Transition Network (also called the Transition Movement). This aims to raise awareness of Peak Oil and climate change, and to prepare people for their implications.

The first Transition Initiative emerged in Totnes in 2006. Since that time, a wide body of shared knowledge, experience and materials have been created. These include a great website at transitionnetwork.org.

Each Transition Initiative is 'dedicated to the creation of tangible, clearly expressed and practical visions' for moving its community 'beyond its present-day dependence on fossil fuels'.[47] To this end, each Initiative is developing its own 'Energy Descent Plan' (EDP). These set out a 20 year 'Plan B' for their community that considers how it 'might transition away from its current oil dependency, and towards a low carbon, resilient way of working'.[48] Practical measures already being taken to help implement EDPs include the establishment of local 'insulation clubs' to assist households to reduce the energy they require for heating.

Some Transition Initiatives are also setting up community Energy Services Companies (ESCOs) to provide locally-generated power from wind, solar or other alternative energy sources. For example, in South Devon the Totnes Renewable

Energy Society is working on two solar power projects, a wood fuel heating scheme, and the development of a community wind farm that will include the installation of two commercial wind turbines.[49]

THE FOLLY OF SUSTAINABILITY

Along with many of the ideas presented in this book, a future transition to low energy lifestyles is commonly associated with the concept of 'sustainability'. This term entered the popular lexicon in 1987 following the definition of 'sustainable development' by the UN World Commission on Environment and Development (WCED), also known as the Brundtland Commission. In *Our Common Future*, the WCED defined 'sustainable development' as 'development that meets the needs of the present without compromising the ability of future generations to meet their own needs'.[50] In short, sustainability is about living today without compromising tomorrow.

I do not necessarily want to appear at odds with a seminal United Nations commission that produced a great report. Nevertheless, I remain dismayed at the increasingly common obsession of wanting to become 'sustainable', or of trying to achieve 'sustainable development' or even 'sustainable economic growth'. As you may have gathered, I am heavily into environmental issues and had a green mentality long before it started to become fashionable. In particular, I believe that there is an urgent necessity for the human race to engage in more local living, to transition to low energy lifestyles, and to take far more responsibility for the world of tomorrow. But associating such measures with any concept of 'sustainability' or of becoming entirely 'sustainable' just makes my blood boil.

My concern is two-fold. Firstly, while the introduction of the term 'sustainability' has made some people think about environmental issues (and I have run workshops with the word in the title myself!), I loathe the term and its many derivatives because it is physically impossible for any kind of consumptive activity (such as the practice and survival of human civilization) to actually be 'sustainable'. Indeed, a physical certainty called the Second Law of Thermodynamics tells us that no closed system – even one as big as a planet – can last forever. The resources available on the Earth are after all finite, constantly depleting, and will all eventually completely run out. We should therefore at best talk about trying to become 'more sustainable', or perhaps about 'responsible living' or something like that.

No individual and no organization can live or function today without compromising the world of tomorrow. Life is a degenerative timeshare, with each of our existences inevitably having some level of detrimental impact on those who may inhabit the planet after us. Our goal should therefore be to leave things in the best state we can for those to come. Anybody who tells you that they are working toward becoming truly 'sustainable' really does not understand the meaning of the term.

You may perhaps consider my objection to 'sustainability' on thermodynamic and linguistic grounds to be self-indulgent nit-picking. Well OK, you may also be right! After all, we all *know* that 'sustainability' is used as a convenient catch-all label for being green and looking after the planet. So what is the problem? Well, my other far more practical objection is that the use and abuse of the term risks fuelling the common if dangerous delusion that there is no need for radical change.

The terms 'sustainable' and 'sustainability' have now been hijacked by a great many politicians and academics who not only do not understand their meaning, but who clearly have no intention of changing their ways. For example, I was recently interviewed by a very influential professor of sustainability who spends his life flying around the world asking people how we can all become more sustainable. Well, for a start, he could substitute e-mail, Skype and other web tools in the place of quite so many airline tickets.

Academics as a species travel far too much to say far too little, and usually achieve even less. Holding meetings and making formal presentations may sometimes be effective tools in any bid to fix the world. But most meetings and presentations can now be conducted electronically in a very proficient manner that does not burn up barrel after barrel of aviation fuel. Fixing the world is not something to be studied, but a job to be done. Just as so many academics and politicians started talking about e-business in the late 1990s when it became the vogue, so today a great many are now bolstering their résumés and manifestos with the new popular darling of 'sustainability'. Given the seriousness of the situation we face, this really is not helpful as false prophets have a tendency to both waste a lot of time and cause a lot of damage.

The more that those in apparent authority talk about 'sustainable this' and 'sustainable that', the greater the risk that the wider population will be fooled into believing that we can all go on living just as we do today, if with a clever, new sustainability dimension added. To return to the point I made at the start of this chapter, the sustainability brigade are already beginning to convince the population that alternative energy sources will be able to help us go on living pretty much as we do today. Running out of oil? No problem. We can simply switch to those nice renewable (read 'sustainable') forms of power. However, as we have seen, due to the far lower net energy yields of all major forms of alternative energy, this will not and cannot work.

Feel the need for the constant economic growth that politicians and their economist buddies seem to believe is essential? Well no problem! We will just continue to consume more and more energy and resources, but in a nice, new eco-friendly 'sustainable' way. This delusion is also utter rubbish as I hope you are aware. Today, far too many politicians and companies get away with 'greenwashing' people into believing that things are environmentally responsible or advantageous when they are not. And this dubious practice is something that far more people need to start recognizing and fast.

The only way to fix the world is for mass humanity to radically change its ways. This does not mean that we need to junk every aspect of how we currently live. But at the very least we need to find ways to consume significantly less stuff and to migrate to new ways of living that use far less power. There really can be no escaping the fact that low energy lifestyles have to involve new ways of going about our daily activities and running our organizations that will be quite different from what most people do today. This will involve radical changes in our collective culture and a mindset shift for the majority. Will the transition be painful? Most certainly. But we really have no choice.

* * *

AN EVOLUTIONARY BLIP

Today, it is incredibly difficult to imagine a previous age in which almost all machines were powered by human muscle or a domesticated animal. And yet, barely 300 years ago, coal, wood, peat and oil were at best used to provide heat and light. Three centuries back, steam power was also virtually unknown, internal combustion engines did not exist, electricity generation was no more than a novelty, and only a madman would have talked of flying or splitting the atom. Our fairly recent ancestors would therefore be amazed that today most of us share our homes and workplaces with a myriad of artificially-powered machines.

The modern age is an incredibly distinct blip in evolutionary history. A few centuries back something magical happened, and that something was the invention of technologies that could generate motion and subsequently electricity from fossil fuels. Since that time we have put our collective foot to the floor in an apparent attempt to extract and consume as many fossil fuel reserves as possible. As a consequence, in a few scant centuries we have burnt up literally hundreds of millions of years of stored photosynthesis. In a sense, the human race has acted like a child who has discovered a single box of chocolates, started to eat them rapidly, and somehow assumed that they can go on stuffing their face forever. But this cannot be the case.

Our transition to low energy lifestyles is a future inevitability that will take place on a great many levels. For a start it will require investments in new corporate and domestic hardware that consumes far less power. Some such lower power devices already exist, while a great many more will be invented as the challenges of Peak Oil, falling net energy yields and climate change become more and more widely understood.

While new technology will be able to lend a hand in increasing our collective energy efficiency, far more important will be increasing our collective energy awareness and altering mindsets so that the average human being seeks to consume less power. As discussed in the last chapter, the transition to more local living will help us on the journey to a low energy lifestyle by reducing our requirement for petroleum, and by decreasing the energy-intensity of our food and other purchased goods. Yet on top of such radical changes, there are lots and lots of little lifestyle alterations that we will all also need to make.

Most of us could start to lead a lower-energy lifestyle by making a few very small changes. Such measures include not overfilling a kettle, minimizing the time we keep a refrigerator door open, using a microwave rather than a conventional oven, turning off our wireless Internet routers when we are asleep or out at work, washing-up in a sink rather than loading a dishwasher, not leaving electronic appliances on 'standby', choosing to walk or cycle rather than taking a bus, travelling on public transport rather than in a private car, favouring trains over planes, and so on. Slightly more radical changes may involve heating and cooling fewer rooms in our homes and workplaces (and in time moving to smaller buildings), eating less cooked food, favouring staycations over foreign holidays, and visiting people outside of our locality less often by increasing our use of online communications tools. I could go on and on with this list, but I am sure you get the point.

In a sense, we need to start living our lives as if we were on an expedition with finite supplies, and with an associated constant awareness that we need to monitor what we consume and make every little bit of energy count. We also need to keep old, less resource-intensive technologies and skills alive, and to learn to accept being a bit less productive if in the process we can save a great deal of power. In essence our choice is very simple: either we find ways to do things with far less energy, or we must prepare to wave goodbye to the Industrial Age.

For many, the prospect of transitioning to a low energy lifestyle may seem both daunting and depressing. It is therefore worth noting that in some parts of the world the process has very much begun. As has been discussed, activists in many countries have already started to form Transition Initiatives to help their communities prepare for Peak Oil and the implications of climate change. Some of the richest countries in the world are also investing heavily in signature projects. For example, the United Arab Emirates is building a new city called Masdar. This is intended as 'a model for [more] sustainable development regionally and globally', and is seeking to deliver 'the highest quality living and working environment with the lowest possible ecological footprint' in a 'community where cutting-edge cleantech research and development, pilot projects, technology testing, and construction on some of the world's most sustainable buildings are all ongoing'.[51]

While in Masdar City the future is being invented and built as a living experiment, across the world in Cuba a low energy lifestyle has been drastically imposed. Following the collapse of the Soviet Union in 1991, Cuba suddenly stopped receiving tankers of oil and $6 billion of aid a year from its communist ally. With very little warning, oil use in Cuba was reduced by 50 per cent in one year. Faced with this situation, the country's 11 million inhabitants had no choice but to very rapidly transition to far less energy-intensive lifestyles. As some have argued, most people in Cuba became 'modernized peasantry', with many forced to 'regress' to a far more agricultural way of life.

With opportunities to use powered machinery significantly reduced, Cuba decided to invest in people by making healthcare and education its priorities. The country went through Hell and back – with an 85 per cent drop in its GDP and the average person losing 20 pounds in weight – but has survived. Private cars are now a luxury, while industrial and petrochemical farming have been replaced by organic growing. But the economy is recovering, with food production restored to 90 per cent of 1990 levels, and a low energy lifestyle now deeply entrenched as the norm.[52]

Few in Cuba will even talk of the 'special period' they went through in the early 1990s, and it is obvious why. But the stark and drastic case study of the country's recent history ought to be a lesson and a wake-up call for us all. Today, only a relatively few individuals can find the motivation to become involved in a Transition Initiative or to take even small measures to start making their lives less energy intensive. Yet I would place a very safe bet that many people would be far happier to engage in these activities than to live through a drastic transition to a low energy lifestyle like the Cubans did. We all have personal choices to make. And, if we want even a relatively soft landing, we need to start making them sooner rather than later.

3

DEMATERIALIZATION

Life is a physically consumptive process. Without food and water we rapidly die, while without clothing, shelter, energy and healthcare we die sooner and live less comfortably. It is therefore inevitable that every one of us will always live a somewhat materialistic lifestyle.

While we cannot live without robbing the planet of at least some of its riches, one of the most obvious ways to fix the world is for all of us to consume less stuff. After all, the less we farm, extract from the ground, burn and bury in a landfill, the less resource-poor and polluted the Earth will become. The less we physically consume today, the more opportunities we will also leave on the table for people in the future.

As discussed in the previous two chapters, we can start to transition to a less materialistic existence by embracing more local living and adopting lower energy lifestyles. Each of these interrelated measures will reduce our physical resource intensity. But we will also need to go far further. As noted in the Prologue, if we do not change our ways then by 2050 human civilization will demand almost three times the physical resource inputs that it consumes today, and such quantities of raw materials will simply not be available.

Only a few generations ago most people consumed far less and reported similar levels of happiness. The problem is that the developed world has become increasingly prone to what psychologists term 'Hedonic adaptation'.[53] This means that we have got used to demanding more, obtaining more, but then attaching less and less value to things almost as soon as we have them.

Consider, for example, the modern marvel of the smartphone. In terms of absolute functionality, every single model on the market is an amazing communications and entertainment device that many people in years gone by would have been thrilled to own. So why is it that so many people hanker after a handset upgrade scant months after getting a new phone?

The answer is that features and functionality that initially seem almost magical are rapidly integrated into our lives and soon become run-of-the-mill. That, or we let corporate marketing departments succeed far too easily in convincing us that we should not be satisfied with what they sold us a year or even a month ago. Either way, we simply cannot go on constantly demanding new stuff when the things we own still work perfectly well. Fifty years ago, almost nobody lived a disposable lifestyle like the majority enjoy today, and this is something we really ought to keep in mind.

This chapter reflects on a range of developments that may help us to 'dematerialize' our lives while retaining reasonable levels of prosperity. 'Dematerialization' simply refers to making things less material so that they consume fewer physical resources. Some objects and processes may be able to be dematerialized completely. However, most forms of dematerialization will reduce rather than entirely remove our requirement to physically consume. Most forms of dematerialization are therefore likely to be relative rather than absolute.

In very broad terms, dematerialization can be achieved in four ways. Firstly, we can exploit the increasing range of opportunities to replace physical things with digital substitutes. Secondly, companies can dematerialize their activities by developing and adopting new manufacturing and distribution processes that produce less waste. Thirdly, we could potentially focus less of our economy on physical products, and more of it on people-centric services. And finally, we may actively seek the demise of mass consumerism so that people cease to purchase – or at least purchase so regularly – some of the things that they demand today.

THE ULTIMATE INVENTION?

Back in 2007, Intel published a white paper called *Advancing Global Sustainability Through Technology*. Within, it claimed the microprocessor to be the 'ultimate invention for achieving a [more] sustainable world'. As the company further pronounced, microprocessors are the most 'emission-reducing device ever made', with 'no other device as important' in 'providing answers for our world's issues'.[54]

Intel may naturally be somewhat biased! This caveat noted, they may well also be right. Computing devices and the microprocessors at their core may now consume several per cent of the world's energy output. But the potential that they provide to help save resources and energy is very substantial. Most fundamentally, computer technology directly facilitates dematerialization by permitting physical things to be replaced with digital alternatives. As Intel explains, information and communications technology permit:

> . . . the same or an increased quality and quantity of goods and/or services [to be] created using fewer natural resources (material or energy). Decreased consumption of paper is a good example . . . Compared to reading a newspaper, receiving the news on a [computing device] wirelessly results in the release of 32 to 140 times less carbon dioxide and

several orders of magnitude less nitrogen oxides and sulphur oxides.[55]

Another report from the European Telecommunications Network Operators' Association (ETNO) and the World Wildlife Fund also strongly makes the case for digital dematerialization. As *Saving the Climate @ the Speed of Light* argues, there are already many instances where physical goods and physically-manipulative services are being replaced with digital equivalents. The most obvious include the exchange of e-mails and texts rather than physical letters, and the downloading of music, computer software and video content as an alternative to purchasing physical CD and DVD media.

Examples of digital dematerialization that may less obviously spring to mind include the use of virtual answering machines (where messages are stored on a telecoms provider's systems rather than equipment in the home or office), online billing, online bank statements, digital ticketing, and the completion of online tax forms. Indeed, according to *Saving the Climate @ the Speed of Light*, if 90 million people in Europe completed their annual tax returns online, this would lead to an annual reduction in CO_2 emissions of 91,278 tonnes.[56]

Both of the aforementioned reports point out that travel and in particular business meetings may be digitally dematerialized by switching to video conferencing. *Saving the Climate @ the Speed of Light* even reveals that some companies are already re-labelling their travel departments as 'meeting departments'. The intention is to signal their role as facilitating communication, rather than necessarily the transportation of human beings. One major multinational has even been reported to offer employees low-price alcohol and tobacco products as an incentive to substitute video conferences for airplane tickets. This policy was apparently instigated because some employees were loath to make use of video conferencing for their overseas meetings purely because it prevented them from obtaining duty-free goods at an airport.

DEMATERIALIZATION HARDWARE

Many IT companies are now launching hardware that will enable the increased digital dematerialization of many forms of media. Most significant here may be the continued roll-out of tablets. Apple, Google, Microsoft and Amazon now all have a stake in the growing tablet market, with their iPad, Nexus, Surface and Kindle devices respectively. Since January 2011, Kindle e-books have been outselling traditional paperbacks on Amazon.com.

According to a report from RISI (a leading information provider on 'forest products'), between 2010 and 2015 digital publications read on tablets will replace up to 20 per cent of magazines, books and newspapers consumed in the United States. By 2030, RISI expects the publication of paper-based media to fall by a further 40 to 50 per cent.[57] In anticipation of this trend, major bookshop chains are preparing for an in-store dematerialization revolution. For example, in the United Kingdom, the book chain Waterstones has signed a deal with Amazon that will allow customers to purchase Kindle e-books in their physical stores.[58] Similarly in the United States, Barnes & Noble has launched in-store stations for its Nook e-reader.[59]

As the above examples highlight, digital dematerialization is starting to accelerate, with a growing number of people now obtaining at least some of their messages, music, news, video, books and magazines without being in receipt of anything tangible. Granted, dematerialization will only help to fix the world if the reader and player hardware that is adopted in place of paper and other physical media is appropriately energy efficient and kept in use for a long period of time. This said, it needs to be remembered that every e-book, album and video downloaded saves not only the resources that would have been invested in a physical book, CD or DVD, but in addition those that would have been used in their packaging, storage and transportation. Pile up a year's worth of the newspapers, books, magazines and DVDs that are consumed by many households, and the case for digitally dematerializing at least a proportion of this content is also fairly easily made.

The end-user hardware necessary for digital dematerialization also continues to improve. For example, a company called Plastic Logic is working on a new type of highly flexible electronic paper. Expected on the market within a few years, this will receive information wirelessly, can display moving, high-resolution colour images, and may be rolled-up and carried around like a conventional newspaper. When it comes to market, it is therefore likely to be even more influential than the current generation of tablets and smartphones in persuading people to adopt a more digitally dematerialized lifestyle.[60]

Governments are also starting to migrate public services into the digital realm, with citizens in many nations already encouraged to complete vehicle licensing renewals, passport applications and similar processes online. Web-based consultations with a doctor are even available to some patients. To support such initiatives, the European Union has proposed the creation of a new fund called the Connecting Europe Facility that is intended to pay for a massive roll-out of super-fast broadband services.[61]

MIGRATING TO THE CLOUD

Digital dematerialization can occur at two levels. The first involves the replacement of physical materials with local digital substitutes. For example, music may be downloaded and stored on a smartphone or MP3 player, while download-ed e-books may be stored on a tablet.

The second level of digital dematerialization is more radical, and involves the replacement of physical materials with online access to a cloud-based digital substitute. In this second scenario, a user ends up with no more than the right to access a digital file, rather than their own individual, digital copy of a song, book, document or video.

Cloud-based dematerialization can result in even greater resource savings than local dematerialization, as there is no need for everybody to maintain their own digital archive. For example, users of a service called Spotify access music files that are streamed to them over the Internet in real-time. A popular song does therefore not end up being stored millions of times over on millions of individual devices, so occupying tens of terabytes of physical storage space. Rather, a single file on a Spotify server is shared with everybody who wants access, and takes up only a few megabytes of storage media. The level of dematerialization that occurs when cloud-based services are adopted is therefore substantially greater than that achieved when each user downloads their own local file.

While local digital materialization is all about owning things in a different format, cloud-based dematerialization adds the extra dimension of owning things in a fundamentally different way. It also necessitates the use of a shared public infrastruc-ture. For these reasons, many people currently do not want to further migrate to the cloud. Some people also worry that cloud-based content can only be accessed when a decent Internet connection is available, and at present for some computer users this is a very legitimate concern.

The potential negatives noted, the trend to stream media, store data, run applications and access computer processing power from the cloud is growing. At present the main drivers of cloud computing are a desire to reduce business IT costs (as cloud services are usually purchased on-demand), and the end-user convenience of multi-device access to the same files. However, for human civilization more broadly, probably the key benefit of cloud computing is the potential it presents to achieve a very high level of dematerialization.

In particular, cloud computing offers the opportunity to dematerialize a significant proportion of local computing infrastructure. For example, cloud computing providers like Amazon, Google and Microsoft now permit companies to get rid of their own servers and data centres, and replace them with cloud computing solutions that provide access to server capacity over the Internet.

At present most small- and medium-sized businesses run one or more computer servers, while most larger businesses run their own data centre. Unfortunately, in global resource terms, running lots of relatively small data centres and local server installations is not very efficient. This is because the servers in most companies typically run at maybe 30 per cent of their potential capacity. In contrast, the servers in the extremely large cloud data centres run by cloud providers can run at approaching 80 per cent capacity or more. The carbon footprint of a unit of computing power delivered from the cloud is therefore usually far lower than that delivered by a local server.

The more companies that migrate their IT infrastructure to the cloud, the fewer the number of servers that will need to be built, maintained and powered. Additional economies of scale may also be reaped by cloud vendors, while their customers only have to hire cloud services for the period of time they actually require them. Amazon Web Services, for example, allows its customers to scale up or down their server requirements by the hour. By choosing to cloud compute, companies can therefore at least partially demate-rialize their IT infrastructure. Recognizing the potential, a recent Gartner survey reported that 50 per cent of compa-nies are now planning to move most of their applications and IT infrastructure to the cloud.[62]

Even private individuals have the potential to save resourc-es by downsizing their computer hardware in favour of a cloud alternative. Free cloud office suites like Google Docs (in which this book is being written), as well as many other cloud applications, can now be used on very low power hardware such as netbooks, tablets and the low-energy PCs mentioned in the last chapter. In fact increasingly, with cloud services available, some home users are likely to find that a large-screen smartphone, tablet or netbook is the only computer they require.

Even those who play high-power computer games may start to abandon resource-intensive, energy-guzzling desktop PCs as cloud services improve. Already a company called OnLive offers an on-demand, cloud-based gaming service that permits many of the latest titles to be played on very basic PCs, tablets or even smartphones. Some users may still want to own a high-power PC as a status symbol as well as their means of playing games. But for those who find constant hardware upgrades a frustrating expense, the option to downgrade the equipment they own and just get on with shooting aliens will prove increasingly attractive. Once again this will mean that physical resources are saved.

3 D PRINTING HORIZONS

As outlined in chapter 1, 3D printers create real, solid objects from digital data by building them up in very thin layers. Already 3D printers can output solid objects in a wide variety of materials including many plastics and metals. In fact, the very latest 3D printers from a company called Objet can print over 100 materials in a single print job. Complex, functional objects can therefore be 3D printed comprised of both hard and flexible parts. This apparent magic is achieved by jetting a mix of different photocurable polymers from a 'polyjet matrix' print head. Each layer of the object is solidified by a powerful ultraviolet light immediately after it is printed. By constantly varying the polymer mix, different materials are created in different locations. Already Audi is manufacturing a few of its car parts using Objet 3D printers.

3D printing will help to save resources and so dematerialize industrial output in two ways. Firstly, manufacturing products (or parts thereof) using 3D printers will result in direct raw material savings. Today, many production processes are based on subtractive manufacturing. This means that they start with a solid block of material and remove material from it using processes such as cutting, drilling and lathing. In contrast, 3D printing is an additive manufacturing process that starts with nothing and adds material until an object is complete. The quantity of raw materials wasted in most 3D printing processes is therefore minimal.

Already major manufacturers are seriously investigating the possibilities. For example, Rolls-Royce is leading a project called MERLIN. This is being funded by the European Union, and is working toward the use of 3D printing in the manufacture of civil aircraft engines.[63] The hope is to achieve near to a 100 per cent utilization of raw materials in engine manufacturing processes using techniques including selective laser sintering (SLS) and selective laser melting (SLM). Here very thin layers of a metal powder are laid down on a print bed, with a laser beam used to fuse the granules together where required. Once a part has been printed, all of the loose, unbound power that surrounds it is removed to be used in the next build. Close to a 100 per cent material utilization can therefore be achieved.

Recently I had the opportunity to discuss the potential of 3D printing aircraft engines with some Rolls-Royce engineers. As they enthused, the possibilities for materials savings are very significant. As they explained, using current subtractive methods, the manufacture of a typical 1 tonne aircraft engine consumes up to 6.5 tonnes of metal, most of which ends up on the machine shop floor. In theory, 3D printing processes could therefore reduce the materials wastage on each engine by approaching 5.5 tonnes – or a saving of nearly 85 per cent.

Just down the road from where Rolls-Royce is located in Derby, a team at Loughborough University are developing a large-scale 3D concrete printer.[64] This is part of a Freeform Building Project that is focused on the potential use of additive manufacturing in the production of full-scale building components. The team's printing process extrudes concrete from a computer-controlled nozzle to make building sections in layers. Already components up to 2.5 x 2.5 x 2 metres can be created, with a 1 tonne reinforced architectural piece having already been produced to demonstrate the viability of the process.

3D concrete printing could allow any building an architect can imagine to be printed on site. Perhaps even more significantly, 3D concrete printers can create concrete sections with internal air gaps or honeycomb structures. Again this permits relative dematerialization, as less concrete is required to 3D print a component of a required size and strength. By printing concrete sections with air gaps inside them, the insulation properties of walls and floors can also be improved.

Today, any material poured into a mould – whether it is concrete, plastic or metal – has to set into a totally solid object. But when an object is additively manufactured using 3D printing, this no longer has to be the case. 3D printers can make components that use fewer raw materials purely because many shapes and semi-hollow objects are impossible to create with conventional manufacturing processes. Already a project funded by the United Kingdom Technology Strategy Board, and entitled 'Sustainable product development via design optimization and AdditiVe manufacturING' or 'SAVING', is intent on 'making more with less' by using 3D printing methods in manufacturing. As it explains:

> The project aims to develop lightweight and sustainable products via material design optimization and additive manufacturing (AM) which will significantly save materials and energy consumption in the production of high value products. As an innovative and promising material process technology, AM allows the rapid development of sustainable products through new lightweight material structure technology that utilises functional metal and plastic materials more effectively. It has the potential to produce high value aerospace, medical and engineering parts with minimum material waste and energy input. For certain complex parts, AM process can save up to 90% of the material compared to subtractive machining processes.[65]

Already the SAVING project has successfully printed end-use components from stainless steel and titanium-alloy powders, with the final parts having internal 'cellular lattice' support structures. Such parts therefore consume less material, in addition to being produced by an additive process that creates less waste.

MATERIALIZATION ON DEMAND
In addition to permitting products to be produced using fewer materials, 3D printing also enables 'materialization on demand'. At present, almost all products are manufactured

long before it is known whether a consumer actually wants them or not, let alone where they will finally be required. A great many resources are therefore used up in the transportation of products around the planet, and moving things in and out of storage. A reasonable proportion of the things that are manufactured also never get sold.

As highlighted in chapter 1, 3D printing will allow products to be printed out as close to the customer as possible, so reducing the requirement for long-distance transportation. In effect, objects will be stored and transported in a totally dematerialized digital format, and will only consume precious resources at the point of printout. Many store rooms and stocks of spare parts will therefore be able to be near-totally dematerialized, and replaced with 3D printers that materialize objects on demand. As explained by Janne Kyttanen, the founder of a company that creates all of its products using 3D printers, 'at Freedom of Creation we believe in a future where data is the design product, and where products are distributed in the same way that images and music travel through the Internet'.[66]

Materialization-on-demand may soon even be happening at home. At the time of writing, personal 3D printers like the Cube and the UP! can be purchased for just over $1,000, while open source 3D printers may be constructed by dedicated enthusiasts for considerably less. By the middle of the decade, easy-to-use domestic 3D printers with all of the bugs ironed out ought to be available for a few hundred dollars. These will allow private individuals to print things out in their kitchen, bedroom or garage. They may also start to radically challenge our requirement to possess physical objects in the first place.

Only ten years ago, virtually all photographs were physical. If somebody showed you their holiday snaps, they therefore did so by presenting you with a bundle of hardcopies. For most of the history of photography, such printouts were produced photochemically from negatives. Then came digital cameras and home photo printers. The former have now all but replaced film-based cameras. Photo printers, however, have had less of an impact than many would have expected or hoped, with an increasing proportion of images shared in a purely digital format.

Today, the vast majority of photographs never hit paper. People could print them out on a photo printer at home, in the office, or using all manner of online and high street bureaus. The fact that this happens less and less is not due to a lack of practical and technological opportunities to materialize our images, but largely because we have grown used to handling and owning images in a purely digital format. Seeing an image on a computer, tablet or smartphone is now usually enough, and especially as we know any digital picture can be 'materialized' if we really wanted it to be. In a similar fashion, in the future we may increasingly be satisfied to own at least some objects in a purely digital format that is potentially 3D-printable.

Over the last decade I have produced a lot of computer animation. In the process I have also built up a substantial archive of 3D computer models. Recently, I uploaded two of these to an online bureau called i.materialise to obtain 3D printouts. The process was as simple as transferring my digital files to their website, and waiting a few days for solid, metal objects to be delivered by their courier. At present such a service is not common, and hence my 3D printouts had to be delivered from Leuven in Belgium to Nottingham in the United Kingdom. But more than likely, within a few years I will be able to either print objects on a domestic 3D printer, or visit a high street bureau to get digital files materialized. Fuji is indeed already considering the installation of thousands of 3D printing kiosks at retail locations, and has already showcased a mock-up of what one may look like.[67]

Obtaining printouts of objects that I have previously only owned in a digital format is quite amazing. Suddenly a whole new world has opened up in which my digital archive of hundreds of 3D models – let alone the hundreds of thousands that exist out there on the Internet – have become potentially physical things. Even so, I am not racing to get more things 3D printed. In part this is due to the current cost. I am, however, also already appreciating that there are many 3D models – and potential 3D scans of things – that I will always be happy to possess in a purely digital, totally dematerialized format. OK, so at present I am currently very unusual in owning a digital model archive. But this is unlikely to remain the case.

Just as most people have become comfortable with possessing dematerialized, digital photos, so I strongly suspect that, within a decade, many of us will be content to harbour digital possessions. Of course, we will want to print some things out. Purely digital spanners, cups, cutlery and shoes are of no use to man nor beast. But some of those ornaments and keepsakes that people have on shelves and in their cupboards may well end up being stored in cyberspace alongside our photos, music and video. In other words, the fact that we will be able to 3D print things may actually mean that we rarely do. Or as Niall Hedderman argues in his e-book *Digging a Hole in the Ground*, we will increasingly consume digital products and only materialize them when needed.[68]

Before I finish this section, it is also worth noting that materialization-on-demand is not just a concept associated with 3D printing. Today, books can be printed-on-demand very effectively by machines that can output a single copy of a 300 page paperback in about a minute. In fact, if you are reading this book in hardcopy, the product in your hand was printed-on-demand (or materialized) *after* you ordered it.

When this book was published, there was no initial bulk print run, with no pallets of materialized paper product left waiting in a warehouse in the hope of future sales. Rather, a few final files were uploaded to Amazon's servers to enable hardcopy books to be printed on demand and e-books to be downloaded. As a result, this book never ought to go out of print. More importantly, there will also never be a mass-pulping of surplus copies.

Today, a large proportion of the books and magazines that get printed never actually get sold. In fact, on many occasions a book in your hand will be partnered by at least one other copy that is never purchased. So much is this an issue that major book retailers like WHSmith offer a pulping service to publishers to help them dispose of wasted stock. Print-on-demand is therefore a great means of reducing waste, and so relatively dematerializing the resources that are still usually invested to deliver printed words into your hand.

A GENTLER MODE OF CAPITALISM?

The last few pages have highlighted various means for delivering roughly the same products or experiences using fewer physical resources. In other words, I have focused on how we may embrace dematerialization while maintaining our current pattern of living. Without doubt, such endeavours are likely to prove a good start. But to fix the world, we will also need to embrace more radical modes of dematerialization.

One important option is for humanity to consume fewer resources by changing the balance of what we collectively spend our money on. An economy focused more on the exchange of digital bits, and less on atom-based products, will clearly require fewer raw materials. But so too would an economy in which we spent less on physical objects, and more on human care, community building and the delivery of non-resource-intensive services. In other words, we could transition to a less resource-intensive economy *without decreasing current levels of prosperity* if more of our trade was people-centric rather than product-centric. As noted at the end of the last chapter, when Cuba was confronted with a dramatic reduction in resources in the early 1990s, its successful response was in part to refocus its economy on healthcare and education.

In 1999 I published a book called *Valueware*[69] in which I proposed a transition to a 'gentler mode of capitalism'. As I mused at the time:

> . . . the hard fact of capitalism is that it is self-fuelling. Demand feeds more demand. That's how the system works. Therefore, as long as our markets are geared toward selling physical goods and physically-manipulative services, the more and more resources the human race will continue to consume and to waste. The only 'way out' – beyond opening our horizons to the vastness of space – therefore has to involve a fundamental shift in that type of consumption which we permit to continue to self-feed.[70]

In short, to help fix the world we need to change not how we trade, but what we trade. A high standard of living could be obtained in a new economy in which we all buy and own fewer physical things, but in which we look after our sick and elderly better, spend more time in education, and devote more of our leisure pursuits to consuming media and the arts rather than engaging in retail therapy.

Today, as in 1999, I continue to believe that a potential future in which we are less product-centric and more people-centric may potentially be based on the capitalist model. This is because, in many respects, capitalism really does work. If nothing else, its 'triumph' over communism in the second half of the 20th century suggests this to be the case. There is no doubt that capitalism in its current form has serious detrimental consequences. But once the things we value have a price placed on them, their supply usually goes up and their price falls (at least in relative terms) as entrepreneurs figure out how to make more supply available. To me at least, this suggests that capitalism remains salvageable.

The above observation noted, our present incarnation of capitalism is clearly far from perfect. In particular, I would highlight two major problems. Firstly, capitalism continues to accelerate a mindless and dangerous trade in physical resources that cannot be sustained, and which risks bleeding the biosphere to death. Secondly, capitalism places economic and financial logic above everything else, and this in turn leads to inequality, exploitation, short-term thinking, and a blindness to the consequences of the aforementioned accelerating consumption of physical resources.

These negative aspects of our current mode of capitalism are very severe indeed. If, however, we could all somehow transition to less resource-intensive economic pursuits – and more local living and low energy lifestyles could well prove a catalyst for that – then we could start to address capitalism's ongoing tendency to continually increase our consumption of physical resources. In this sense a form of capitalism that is both gentler on the planet and gentler on ourselves could potentially start to be practised. This still leaves the second major issue of our slavery to short-term economic logic and its dire human consequences. But for now I will leave that as a matter to return to with a vengeance in chapter 7.

RIP Consumer Society

Recently I made one of my rare visits to a large department store. I needed to go there, as my thirteen-year-old washing machine had pretty much given up the ghost and was threatening to flood my kitchen if I turned it on again. With my usual trepidation I therefore crossed the threshold, rode the escalators to the second floor, purchased a replacement appliance, and got out before the distraction of the shiny displays and bright lights could get the better of me. This said, even after my brief and successful mission, I was left with an overwhelming awareness of so many amazing products that I could purchase, but which I really do not need.

So far in this chapter I have highlighted how we may dematerialize our lives by adopting digital substitutes and 3D printing, and by refocusing our economy away from physical products and toward less resource-intensive human services. Yet as we all know, the single easiest and yet most difficult way to achieve a significant level of dematerialization is for every one of us to just start consuming less stuff. OK, so recycling may help a bit, as may keeping things longer and repairing broken items as I will discuss in the next chapter. But there can be no doubt that many of the problems that the world faces today are a result of the relentless rise of the planetary cancer known as mass consumerism. To fix the world we therefore have to reduce the common belief in our divine right and absolute necessity to endlessly consume.

In the last chapter I described the modern age as a tiny blip in evolutionary history. Almost certainly today's practice of mass consumerism is the most distinctive element of that blip. The relentless purchase and exchange of objects now pervades all aspects of most people's lives in developed nations, and not only in the domestic sphere.

Recently I had to clear out my university office in order to relocate to another. The sheer volume of material that I ended up discarding was astounding, and almost everything that I threw away or sent for confidential disposal could have been initially provided to me in a dematerialized format, or never provided at all. Office supply catalogues are as crammed full of things that we do not need as any department store, and unfortunately their pages get the better of many. Having spent over a week removing paper from plastic pockets, folders, box files and all manner of bindings, it became very, very obvious that many offices could save a great deal of space and resources very easily indeed.

The problem I think is two-fold. Firstly, an increasing proportion of the population has grown up in a culture that celebrates the act of purchasing, and which bears no shame every time it throws something away. Secondly, a significant number of people now spend their working lives trying to relentlessly sell us new stuff. As somebody who has worked in a business school for over 20 years, I never cease to be both amazed and saddened at how many business undergraduates want to become marketeers, and how few want to work in product production or service delivery. And no, I really cannot accept that what most marketeers do constitutes the delivery of a 'service'.

In a 2012 report called *Resilient People Resilient Planet: A Future Worth Choosing*, the United Nations High Level Panel on Global Sustainability made some very stark and clear observations. As it noted, 'the current economic model is pushing us inexorably towards the limits of natural resources and planetary life support systems'. We therefore need 'to change dramatically' as 'continuing on the same path will put people and our planet at greatly heightened risk'.[71]

Mass consumerism is very much part of this problem, with the United Nations panel further noting that 'most goods and services sold today fail to bear the full environmental and social cost of [their] production and consumption'. One possible mechanism to curtail the excesses of mass consumerism may therefore be the introduction of new pricing mechanisms that fully reflect all of the costs of making, transporting, marketing and disposing of material goods. Yet without significant transgovernmental agreement and action, this is exceedingly unlikely to happen. Given much of the developed world's current state of austerity, few if any politicians will be willing to impose price increases that would depress their economies further, and which would most likely be criticized as new forms of taxation. More fundamentally, while altered pricing mechanisms could slow mass consumerism, they would not do anything to change its nature.

Persuading people to consume fewer physical things and to value their possessions more is an enormous ask. This said, I have no doubt whatsoever than in 50 years time most people will purchase many products for life, and other things far less – a practice that was common until the middle of the last century. A lack of available resources will simply make a return to such behaviour inevitable. The choice before us today is therefore how we want to arrive back at our old way of living. A smooth transition would of course be preferable. But as long as bankers and marketeers are left in control (and hopefully in the resource-starved world of 20 years hence their kind will have far less influence), the rest of us will have to fight hard to achieve any form of soft landing.

* * *

LIVING WITH LESS STUFF

Forsaking physical possessions has long been the quest of monks, nuns and others of deep faith. More broadly, it could be argued that most religions seek to guide their followers on a journey toward their own dematerialization. In life, all humans lead a physical existence embodied in flesh, bone and blood. On death, most religions believe that the soul journeys to a better place beyond the physical. Heaven, nirvana and other eternal realms therefore all offer us the ultimate in dematerialization.

Consumer society and religious conviction have rarely been good bedfellows. One is principally involved with materialization, while the other has dematerialization as its focus. To be at one with the natural world, it ought also to be fairly obvious that we need to focus far less on physical possessions and the consumption of natural resources.

All matter in the Universe is at best on loan. Each of us borrows a few trillion atoms and imbues them with our sentience for our brief period alive. During that time, many people then seemingly compete to obtain as many things as humanly possible. In part such actions may be foisted upon us by a culture that marks us as different if we question the ideology of mass consumerism. But culture is also something that we can individually influence, change and control. As I argued in the Prologue, each of our actions matters, and hence we all have a role to play in the pursuit of collective dematerialization. Every thing we choose not to needlessly consume – or to consume in a more dematerialized format – really can make a difference.

Last week I was on a train to London. During the journey the train manager (they used to be called guards or conductors) came along to sell and check tickets. When this occurred, a woman on the table next to mine was deep in conversation on her smartphone. To my amazement, she managed to purchase a ticket, and to obtain return journey details, without even a pause in her conversation. It struck me that today this is probably not unusual, with many people having learnt to mentally dematerialize themselves so that their immediate physical circumstances no longer impede their thoughts, actions or interactions. On one level this is socially questionable. But on another it may prove to be the start of something very significant. To help fix the world, we may only need to further heighten some people's growing ability to dematerialize their activities via a partial emigration to the digital realm.

Some may question whether those who already part-reside in cyberspace are actually leading the way. But what is not in doubt is that at least some level of dematerialization will soon be vital for the continued successful functioning of our civilization. Or as John Michael Greer puts it so well in *The Long Descent*, on the far side of the Peak Oil curve, our capacity to survive will largely depend on the number of physical things we can do without.[72]

4

DESIGN FOR REPAIR

The other day my kettle blew up. Well OK, it did not actually explode. But it did make a couple of very strange clicking noises, and then refused to warm up ever again.

Not that many years ago, when a kettle stopped working most people bought a new heating element and fitted it themselves. Those unable or unprepared to engage in a little DIY alternatively took the broken kettle to an electrical store where somebody replaced the element for them. Either way, the bulk of the kettle survived to boil another day. It is therefore rather sad that, in more recent times, it has become pretty much impossible to replace the heating element in most domestic kettles.

The base of my particular kettle was factory-sealed to prevent user access. Even if I had got inside – and I did consider it! – I would not have been able to obtain a replacement for the burnt-out element. I therefore had to discard the entire appliance and replace it with a new one. (For similar reasons I had to say goodbye to the broken washing machine I mentioned in the last chapter as components were unavailable or uneconomic to obtain).

Most manufacturers will tell you that making a kettle with a replaceable element is more expensive than making one with no user-serviceable parts. In their further defence, they may also argue that kettles are now so cheap that there is no point in anybody wasting their precious time repairing one. In the long run, however, it would save both money and scarce planetary resources if we returned to an age in which kettles and many other products could be mended when they went wrong. Almost certainly a repairable kettle would cost a little more. But after just one change of heating element, the extra cost would be more than recouped. We may also start to take better care of our possessions – and to appreciate them more – if we began to invest a little personal time in their maintenance.

AKIN TO CHILD LABOUR

So far in this book I have presented three broad measures that a great many people or businesses could implement to help build a better future. In contrast, this chapter is a little different. Herein I am going to focus on a narrow but important matter under the direct control of a relatively small number of product manufacturers. This issue is 'design for repair', and could remove our regular requirement to dispose of so many things when just one or a few of their components break or wear out.

As I have detailed already in this book, almost all of us squander too many natural resources and burn up far too much energy. Often we could directly choose to do something about this. But when something that we own breaks or wears out, we are often forced to replace rather than repair it because the manufacturer has set this course of action in stone at the design stage.

Most manufacturers are more than capable of designing products that could be repaired, and that would then last far, far longer. Of course, they may not wish to do this as it may lead them to sell less stuff (although a new market in spare parts and maintenance would emerge). As highlighted in the last chapter, there is also the problem that mass consumer culture has made constant product disposal and replacement not just *acceptable*, but often *desirable*. Most people want a constant stream of new things, rather than older things that get mended. Manufacturers may therefore argue that, in making non-repairable products with designed-in obsolescence, they are simply responding to the market. To make companies listen, we therefore need to turn the design of non-repairable products into something that is considered as unethical as exploiting child labour, destroying rain forests, or hacking phones.

A rising number of consumers are starting to turn away from businesses whose supply chains rely on practices that they consider to be unacceptable. Many retailers are now not just aware of this, but intent on the implementation of strict controls to ensure that they and their suppliers all act in an ethical manner. For example, some retailers try to guarantee that none of their clothing is produced in sweatshops, that the tuna in their tins is dolphin friendly, and that the farmers who grow their tea or cocoa are paid a fair wage.

The growing trend for ethical consumerism is already having an impact on what some companies make and supply. While manufacturers may always remain in direct control of design decisions, it is therefore quite possible that design for repair could be indirectly championed via the actions of ethical consumers. We simply need to get the creation of non-repairable items added to the list of those things that are starting to be considered unacceptable.

To help design for repair to enter the mainstream, more and more people just need to start asking the question 'when it goes wrong, which parts can be replaced?' If this query starts to be raised often enough and loudly enough, then design for repair will begin to influence organizational practice, and in turn the products we can all buy.

A New Relationship

It took me some time to settle on the title for this chapter. Designing as many products as possible so that they can be repaired when they go wrong would certainly save resources. But so too could many other popular green initiatives. My final decision to champion 'design for repair' was therefore taken not only to highlight a resource saving measure, but more importantly to signal a way to fix the world that may fundamentally change our relationship with things. In comparison to several other more widely discussed environmental measures, design for repair is critical in any such change as it involves a broad reassessment of product lifecycles.

Today, very few consumer goods last – or are intended to last – more than five years. As a consequence, between 20 and 50 million tonnes of circuit boards, batteries and other e-waste alone are disposed of globally every year.[73] Much of this could be avoided if products such as smartphones, televisions and tablets were designed with repair in mind, and without the assumption that they only had to keep working for a few years.

To explain why design for repair is so important, we first need to consider alternative methods that could help us to save resources. Beyond more local living, low energy lifestyles and dematerialization, these most obviously include recycling, and the second use rather than disposal of unwanted goods.

To start with the latter, today nobody should even think of putting a functional item in a bin if somebody else could make use of it. Taking the effort to pass on useful items for second use is something that almost everybody can do at some point in their lives. It has indeed been common practice within families and circles of friends for generations, as well as a mainstay of charity shops.

Thankfully, freely putting unwanted items into second use is starting to become easier and easier. Not least, the online initiative Freecycle is proving very successful in connecting those who harbour unwanted possessions with others locally who need them. Or as the Freecycle Network proclaims on behalf of its 5,000+ groups and nine million members, its goal is to change the world one gift at a time.[74]

In addition to increasing the reuse of unwanted items, recycling is now very popularly promoted as a means of saving resources. Often this involves the separation of paper, plastics, metals and other fairly basic materials from general domestic or business waste. Any such activity is to be applauded provided that the isolated items actually end up being usefully reclaimed without too much energy being spent. Also of significant benefit is the separation of organic waste. At the very least this prevents organic materials festering in landfills, and in ideal circumstances can provide a raw material for anaerobic digestion. However, these points noted, recycling is certainly not the environmental panacea that many promote it to be or wish it to become.

Not least, in most instances recycling could be more accurately referred to as 'downcycling'. In other words, the act of recycling usually results in a reusable material of a lower quality than the original. For example, when different plastics are recycled they are all mixed together to produce a low-quality hybrid with a more limited number of applications. The same occurs when most metals are recycled. For example, as Michael Braungart and William McDonough explain:

> . . . the high-quality steel used in making automobiles – high-carbon, high-tensile steel – is 'recycled' by melting it down with other car parts, including copper from the cables in the car, and the paint and plastic coatings. These materials

lower the recycled steel's quality. More high-quality steel may be added to make the hybrid steel strong enough for its next use, but it will not have the material properties to make new cars again. Meanwhile, the rare metals, such as copper, manganese, and chromium, and the paints, plastics and other components that had value for industry in an unmixed, high-quality state are lost.[75]

As the above explanation makes very clear, recycling is far from an optimal response to our excessive consumption of resources and premature product disposal. In particular it needs to be appreciated that the more complex an item, the less effective recycling becomes. A level up from the largely beneficial separation and recycling of plastics and metals from general waste, the increased recycling of more complex items – from kettles and irons, to televisions, computers, mobile phones, vehicles and all manner of other appliances – is therefore something that we really ought to seriously question. There is simply no technology or no magic button currently available that can turn many of the things we are finished with into pristine raw materials.

Recycling does undoubtedly have its merits. But it at best remains a sub-optimal solution that has somehow metamorphosed into modern civilization's get-out-of-jail-free card and the latest feel-good craze. Indeed, for many people, recycling appears to have become the penance they are prepared to pay in exchange for feeling better about a throwaway lifestyle. It is therefore unfortunate that, in common with other green illusions like carbon trading, recycling simply does not address our cultural requirement for radical change.

In their book *Use Less Stuff*,[76] Robert Lilienfeld and William Rathje capture the essence of the problem perfectly. As they analogize, today recycling has become like an aspirin taken to try and alleviate the rather large hangover that results from our collective over-consumption. Taking more and more aspirin will not make the problem go away, and indeed may eventually kill us. Whether we like it or not, our only sensible long-term strategy is to consume things less rather than recycling things more.

BEYOND CRADLE-TO-CRADLE

The critique of recycling provided in the previous section is particularly important because, over the past couple of decades, an initiative known as 'cradle-to-cradle' manufacturing has become common across some industries. In short, this seeks to optimize the lifecycle of those materials used in a product. The cradle-to-cradle approach therefore requires designers to consider not just how something is going to be made and used, but additionally how it may be taken apart and its materials 'recycled' at the end of its working life. I would strongly stress the word 'may' here, as cradle-to-cradle initiatives are only as effective as the final actions of end consumers. Today, many items – such as batteries and low-energy light bulbs – bear a symbol that states that they cannot be disposed of in a conventional bin. But this does not stop a fair proportion of us consigning them to landfill or offering them up for incineration.

Cradle-to-cradle initiatives do, I suppose, raise designer and manufacturer awareness of the future rubbish they are creating. However, I still worry that they focus far too heavily on making products that customers will still fairly rapidly discard, rather than on creating things that can be used for years and years with careful maintenance and occasional repair. In other words, cradle-to-cradle tries to change either end of the manufacturing and disposal value chain, rather than seeking to alter how long a consumer may own and maintain a functional product.

As I noted at the start of this chapter, far too often we throw away nearly-functional items because they either cannot be repaired, or because they are uneconomic to repair. None of this is inevitable, as it rarely happened 50 plus years ago. Cradle-to-cradle basically addresses this issue by saying, 'hey, let's continue to throw away as much stuff as we do today, but let's try to feel better about it by supposedly recycling more of what we discard'. Such an approach clearly represents some level of improvement. But it really does not address the two critical problems of our disposable society and our fundamentally broken relationship with things.

The recycling industry already burns vast quantities of oil to move hundreds of thousands of tonnes of junk around the globe every year. It also creates vast legal and illegal rubbish tips that scar and pollute human settlements and the planet. It would therefore be far, far better if we started demanding and designing products that can be maintained for long periods, rather than accepting the recycling and cradle-to-cradle con-trick that is being sold to us by manufacturers and governments who want endless mass consumerism to continue unabated.

PCs, DVDs & BATH PLUGS

Just before we get too gloomy, it is worth noting that not everything we purchase is doomed for disposal once a part of it fails. For example, desktop computers contain a great many components that can be fairly easily replaced. For many years, new microprocessors, memory chips, graphics cards, hard disks, optical drives, fans and power supplies have been regularly substituted for broken parts in the hundreds of millions of PCs that are now liberally scattered across businesses and homes. Granted, more modern computing form factors like tablets, smartphones and ultrabooks (thin laptops) are more difficult and sometimes impossible to repair. Even so, many a designer could learn some useful lessons from a study of desktop computer hardware and the way in which it has been designed for upgrade and repair.

An interesting comparison to make is with consumer audio-visual equipment. Take DVD or hard disk video recording units as an example. These decode a TV signal from an aerial, cable or satellite and record the output. In effect, DVD or hard disk recorders are just single-function domestic computers, and indeed share their recording media and many other components with desktop PCs. They therefore ought to be easy to repair. And yet they are not.

If the DVD drive fails on a desktop PC it can be easily replaced. A standard drive mechanism is usually fitted in under half an hour, and everything continues just fine. In contrast, if the DVD drive fails in a dedicated video recording unit then the whole product has to be scrapped. Why? Because Sony, Panasonic, Samsung and their ilk do not use standard optical disk mechanisms in domestic video recording units. Given that these are the most likely part of the product to fail, this is scandalous. Most manufacturers of domestic video recording units even make standard DVD drives for use in personal computers! There is absolutely no reason that they could not use these in their domestic video recording hardware. They simply choose not to do so in order to prevent their products from being repaired.

Even more surprisingly, it is often extremely difficult to replace the hard disk in many consumer video recording devices. Here standard hard disks – identical to those used in desktop PCs – are always fitted. But manufacturers of video recorders program the internal software (or firmware) of their devices so that only exact disk models can be used. Because hard disk specifications are subject to constant improvement, this means that by the time the drive fails in a video recording unit, finding a replacement hard disk that the unit will accept is somewhat difficult and often impossible. Again, there is absolutely no technical reason why the hard disk in a video recorder cannot be replaced. The problem is purely that manufacturers pre-configure their hardware to prevent repair.

The above is another disgrace that most consumers unthinkingly accept. Millions of video recording devices with perfectly good cases, power supplies, circuit boards and displays get disposed of every year when their hard drive fails and cannot be exchanged for a new one. This is also something that most people would not put up with in other aspects of their lives.

Last year my bath plug literally came apart in my hand as I was pulling it out to let the water drain away. Did I then have to purchase another bath? Of course not! A trip to the hardware store, and they sold me a new plug for 25 pence. If I had been required to rip out and replace the whole bath it would have been considered absolutely crazy. But this is only because disposable consumer culture has yet to go quite that far. If we continue at the rate we are going, then every time a tap starts dripping we may need to get a new bathroom fitted. What is more, if the marketeers are allowed to continue to have their way, many people may even *want* to wallow in such throw-away, resource-wasting and expensive newness every time a washer needs changing.

EMBRACING THE PRACTICALITIES

To save dwindling planetary resources – and also to save consumers money – it is time for designers worldwide to change their ways. Granted, consumer attitudes and skillsets also need to change. But for now I will put that issue to one side, and focus on the key practicalities that many businesses need to embrace.

Humanity has to be approaching that key moment when we stop designing rapid obsolescence into so many things. Or as sustainable design pioneers Michael Braungart and William McDonough contend:

> ... at some point a manufacturer or designer [needs to decide], "We can't keep doing this. We can't keep supporting and maintaining this system." At some point they [must] decide that they would prefer to leave behind a positive design legacy. But when is that point?

> We say that point is today, and negligence starts tomorrow. Once you understand the destruction taking place, unless you do something to change it, even if you never intended to cause such destruction, you become involved in a strategy of tragedy. You can continue to be engaged in that strategy of tragedy, or you can design and implement a *strategy of change.*[77]

So what does such a 'strategy of change' look like? Well, for a start, designers need to start creating products that are as simplified and modular in their construction as possible. Simple designs are inevitably easier to repair, while devices built from modular pieces can be taken apart easily and their components replaced like Lego.

The standardization of as many parts, connectors, screws and other fixing methods as possible can also help considerably. Standardized, modular design is after all what makes desktop PCs so easy to repair. Manufacturers can also increase possibilities for repair by using the same specialist parts and assemblies across as wide a proportion of their product range as possible. This allows repair technicians to become more familiar with parts, as well as increasing the chances of spares being available.

It is also important for designers to label and number the parts that make up a product, and to provide particularly good access to those components that are most likely to break or wear out.[78] Batteries glued deep inside a casing, rather than clipped between sprung contacts behind a surface panel, are increasingly common and yet a powerful example of what needs to change.

Additionally critical in design for repair is a careful consideration of how and why a product may need to be taken apart after its initial manufacture. As argued by the designer and creative director Alex Diener, designers need to start asking themselves questions such as 'which parts of a product are most likely to need replacement?', 'who could potentially repair the product when it breaks or parts wear out?', and 'how can product disassembly and repair be turned into an experience that is simple and intuitive?'

Alex goes on to point out that products that are easy to take apart and repair are often also the easiest to assemble in the first place. Products that are designed for repair will therefore save manufacturers time and money. Alex is also keen to stress that all designers ought to expect their products to have many users. These include not just those people who will own the working item, but also future service personnel or DIY enthusiasts who may end up repairing the product or recycling at least some of its components.[79]

For too long it has been acceptable for designers to create things that are very difficult to disassemble, almost always uneconomic to repair, and usually emblazoned with the label 'no user serviceable parts inside'. The latter is no more than a lazy design cop-out that has to be addressed. As natural resources dwindle and austerity continues, both smart and cash-poor consumers will increasingly be asking 'why are there no user serviceable parts inside?' and 'why is this thing held together with glue or non-standard fastenings that stop me even investigating if repair is a possibility?'

I am in no way suggesting that every single product can or should be serviceable by the average consumer in their own home. For safety reasons, some items – such as medical devices, vehicles and high-voltage electrical products – ought always to repaired by experts (although expertise is something that anybody may acquire). This said, at present many of the things we buy cannot be repaired by anybody! Not least this is because replacement parts are not even made available. This is clearly something that designers and manufacturers can start to do something about right away.

In time, the 3D printers mentioned in previous chapters ought to be able to printout replacement components for many products from online digital archives. However, even when this can happen, clear repair instructions, effective part labelling and good design-for-disassembly will need to become standard practice to enable replacement parts to be successfully fitted.

To help promote the cause, *Make Magazine* – a publica-tion that 'unites, inspires, informs, and entertains a growing community of resourceful people who undertake amazing projects in their backyards, basements, and garages' – has created a 'Maker's Bill of Rights' for accessible, extensible and repairable hardware.[80] Its authors start with the very simple philosophy that 'if you can't open it, you don't own it'. And with this I heartily agree. Designers and manufac-turers really ought to stop expecting their customers to purchase sealed magic boxes that have to be sent to the mysterious land of disposal city within a few years. To this end, the 'Maker's Bill of Rights' succinctly captures many of the points included in this section, and is reproduced in full as Figure 4.1.

Fortunately, there is now at least some evidence that major manufacturers are starting to take notice. For example, in

makezine.com

THE MAKER'S BILL OF RIGHTS

- Meaningful and specific parts lists shall be included.
- Cases shall be easy to open. ■ Batteries shall be replaceable. ■ Special tools are allowed only for darn good reasons. ■ Profiting by selling expensive special tools is wrong, and not making special tools available is even worse. ■ Torx is OK; tamperproof is rarely OK.
- Components, not entire subassemblies, shall be replaceable. ■ Consumables, like fuses and filters, shall be easy to access. ■ Circuit boards shall be commented.
- Power from USB is good; power from proprietary power adapters is bad. ■ Standard connectors shall have pinouts defined. ■ If it snaps shut, it shall snap open. ■ Screws better than glues. ■ Docs and drivers shall have permalinks and shall reside for all perpetuity at archive.org. ■ Ease of repair shall be a design ideal, not an afterthought. ■ Metric or standard, not both.
- Schematics shall be included.

Make:
technology on your time

Drafted by Mister Jalopy, with assistance from Phillip Torrone and Simon Hill.

Figure 4.1: The Maker's Bill of Rights
Drafted by Mister Jalopy with assistance from Phillip Torrone & Simon Hill.
Reproduced with permission of Makezine.com.

October 2011 the US Patent & Trademark Office published a patent application from Apple that includes a variety of new designs for portable devices that would be easier to repair.[81] Options being entertained include cover assemblies that may hinge or slide aside to allow some components to be replaced.

As another very significant example, the Research Council for Automobile Repairs (RCAR) has established a Repairability Working Group. This has already published an extensive design guide for manufacturers that highlights good design practice for repairability and damage limitation. This 90 page document is freely available online, and details how opportunities for cost-effective repairs may be improved in every part of a vehicle. Topics covered include optimal material choices, the order of overlapping body panels, the choice of welding and other fixing methods, and ensuring adequate access to allow inspectors to assess and approve the safety of repairs.[82]

A RETURN TO THE OLD WAYS

While it is the job of designers and manufacturers to deliver a new generation of repairable products, all of us need to be prepared to change our ways when they come to market. There is, after all, a strong possibility that those with sufficient personal resources could continue to discard broken yet repairable items. As I have already indicated, our throwaway, consumer society is a big part of the problem. Or as designer Mike Elam argues in a great article on design for repair, 'we've become so obsessed with the "new" that disposal doesn't bother us'.[83]

Rather than turning down our noses at the idea of 'putting up with things that have been mended', we need to remind ourselves that repair is one of the most natural things in the world. For a start, nature excels at self repair. The whole science of medicine – a rising focus for our economy and arguably humankind's greatest achievement – is also a repair-focused discipline. So why, over the past 50 years, has product repair been allowed to drop so far down our list of priorities?

The answer, as on so many occasions, lies with our addiction to economics, and is specifically linked to the profitability inherent in mass production. Today, it is relatively easy for a manufacturer to build a factory that can churn out thousands of identical products every hour or day, and from which they may earn a healthy economic return. In contrast, it remains impossible to create a highly-automated facility capable of product repair.

Even when manufactured items naturally wear out, they break in different ways. Almost every broken item therefore presents a slightly different repair challenge. It is also far easier to deliver shiny, new parts to a production line for assembly, than it is to create a system capable of disassembling, diagnosing, repairing and reassembling used goods. This all means that while product manufacture is an increasingly technology-centric activity that can be highly automated, repair is very much a person-centric craft and will probably remain so.

Because repair is difficult to automate, it remains an expensive service for most companies to offer. It is indeed for this reason that so many products – from irons and microwaves to MP3 players, printers, cameras and even vehicles – are so often uneconomic to repair. In pure financial terms, it simply costs more to get somebody to open them up than it does for a factory to churn out a new item. In time, and as resources get scarcer and localization overtakes globalization, this situation is bound to reverse. Even so, repair will remain an individually practised human activity.

What the above implies is that, to reap the potential benefits of design for repair, many of us will need to relearn old craft skills. This absolutely does not mean that *everybody* will have to know how to mend things. Yet all of us will need to start valuing repair as a critical craft skill within our local communities. This will require changes in our education system, as well as an attitude shift back in favour of those who like to tinker and mend. To again cite designer Mike Elam:

> We no longer value the kind of practical skills our grandparents would have considered essential to daily life. For example, how many of us who own a bicycle will take it down to the local bike shop to have a puncture repaired rather than attempt the task ourselves? We are losing even the most basic maintenance skills, and with them the thrill and satisfaction we get from fixing things and doing something practical with our hands. We've also forgotten what attachment means. We place less and less emotional value on the objects we populate our lives with. We lose the concept of familiarity and come to expect constant change and upheaval.[84]

As Mike suggests, the fact that our belongings are becoming more transient is also something that we cannot ignore and which needs to change. As I have repeatedly argued, modern society must seriously reassess its relationship with things. There is nothing necessarily wrong with using natural resources to make nice products that give us pleasure or that help us to live more easily. Life is, after all, a physically consumptive process. But we ought to feel ashamed of our throwaway cultural norms. The term 'disposable culture' is overused, and yet really not strong enough. Our recent ancestors would be ashamed of our current attitudes, and rightly so. They used to scrimp and save for things that lasted a lifetime. In contrast today, many people borrow to the hilt for products that are often in the garbage before they are fully paid for.

Of course, not everybody parts company with older and non-functional items when they cease to be of immediate use. As witnessed by the growth of the personal self-storage industry, a substantial minority somehow cannot bring themselves to let go. In fact, self storage in the United Kingdom has boomed in recent years, with over 20 million square feet of storage space now available in warehouses run by Big Yellow, Safestore and their competitors. In the United States, there are a staggering 41,000 self storage warehouses with more than 1.6 billion square feet of space available. Even the sparsely populated Australia has over 1,000 self storage warehouses offering 22 million square feet in which its citizens can hoard.[85]

The fact that people are willing to rent warehouse space in which to store out-of-use items – let alone to fill their sheds, garages, roofs and houses with such possessions – leads me to believe that the problem of over-disposable living is widely recognized. Many people would I think be happy to buy things less and maintain things more. It is just that current design norms do not easily allow this to happen. My hunch is that hoarding will decrease when a greater proportion of products can once again be maintained in good working order for long periods.

EVOLVING OUR STUFF

As people choose or are economically forced to keep things longer and to take far better care of them, so an increasing number of our possessions will slowly evolve. Most people already evolve their homes every time they hang a picture, redecorate, fit a shelf, change a kitchen or bathroom, knock down a wall, or put up an extension. We do not expect to purchase houses and then leave them untouched, and so it ought to be with many other items.

For a couple of decades I have partially earned my living

by talking, writing and making videos about computing. Given this vocation, people are often shocked when they see the PC that I use for video editing and other processor intensive tasks. Its 12-year-old case is very large, yellowed, and has been modified on several occasions. Within are parts of a wide variety of ages, with a few even being descendants of the first PC I ever built back in 1996. Since that time I have had several motherboards blow, many optical drives pack up, and more disks, graphics cards and miscellaneous items in and out of the machine than I can recall. And so my PC has evolved. Sometimes the changes have been made following a decision to upgrade. Though more commonly, new parts have been fitted after something has failed.

The fact that I own a PC that looks like it came out of the Ark, and which has been subject to constant maintenance, makes me somewhat unusual. And that is very sad. As I noted back in chapter 1, Rock's Law informs us that the cost of making microprocessors and other computer components roughly doubles every four years. This means that new products that contain microelectronics (and this means not just computers, but most electrical goods these days) will usually consume more resources in their manufacture than any item they replace. In resource terms, there is therefore a very strong case for design for repair and for our possessions to evolve with us as they are maintained.

It is admittedly sometimes difficult to strike the best balance between running old kit, and replacing it with a new and more energy-efficient device. But in general, we have to start strongly associating the privilege of owning something with a responsibility to keep it in use for as long as reasonably possible. Hopefully in a few years time, my evolving PC will not be quite as unusual as it is today.

* * *

A Ray of Hope

I started this chapter with a personal anecdote about a broken kettle that could not be repaired. I therefore thought it would be nice to draw things to a close with a final personal example of design for repair at its best.

As an old-fashioned kind of filmmaker, I almost always place my camera on a tripod. Sadly last year a leg lock on one of my tripods broke. Immediately I could see that one small, plastic part had split at a pressure point. Given that this had occurred on the smallest and cheapest of my tripods, I immediately assumed that repair would not be possible. But I was wrong.

My tripod was manufactured by Manfrotto, a leading Italian maker of camera supports. To my delight, a visit to manfrottospares.com quickly revealed that every single part of my tripod could be easily identified and purchased online. Manfrotto has long adopted those design for repair practices discussed in this chapter, with its vast range of tripods based around a robust inventory of standardised components. Within a week I therefore had a replacement piece of plastic in my hand.

My only gripe was that the *only* thing in my hand was the replacement part, with no instructions supplied. While the tripod was not that complicated to take apart and its repair required few tools, it was also not immediately obvious how I should proceed. Fortunately, a YouTube search soon led me to a video in which a kind man from somewhere in the United States showed me exactly what to do. An hour later, and my tripod was mended and is still working fine.

The fact that a person from another continent helped me to mend my broken tripod is quite staggering. Yet today it is also run-of-the-mill. Ask a question on the Internet, and the chances are that the best and possibly the *only* answer available will come from a private citizen, rather than a faceless organization.

A growing number of people are now getting very good at using online video and other social media resources to work together, to solve problems, and to help each other out. This activity is known as 'crowdsourcing', and just happens to be the subject of the next chapter.

5

CROWDSOURCING

One afternoon in 1986 I was sitting in a lecture theatre with my fellow undergraduates. In one of the few university classes that I distinctly remember, an aspiring economics professor scribbled differential calculus over several blackboards for nearly an hour. I cannot recall any of the involved mathematics. But I clearly recollect that, by the end of his frantic scribblings, he had apparently proven that if people cooperated the world would be a better place.

I could not and still do not doubt the young professor's conclusion. Yet to this day I remain startled at his need for in-depth calculations to prove the point. It was therefore in 1986 that I started to realize that economic theory is often not worth the chalk dust it is written in. Such thoughts are also not ideal mental fodder for an economics undergraduate!

The folly of economics is a subject to which I will return in the final chapter of this book. But what I want to focus on right now are the still often unexploited benefits of human cooperation. United we have a greater chance of succeeding, while divided we are more likely to fall. It is so blindingly obvious that given chalk and time even an economist can apparently work out that cooperation beats competition.

To capitalize on the benefits that more cooperation may bring, my fifth proposal to fix the world is for an increased uptake of 'crowdsourcing'. This refers to the use of the Internet to help generate value from the contributions of a great many people. Over the past decade or so, tens of thousands of pioneering individuals have begun to link together online in radically new cooperative ways. Sometimes this has been to develop free or low-cost products and services that are not being delivered by traditional, profit-first business organizations. In other instances, it has been to help people out, to spread useful information, or to conduct business in new ways.

The term 'crowdsourcing' was first coined by Jeff Howe in 2006 to refer to new mechanisms for distributed, online problem solving.[86] Since that time, the term has attracted a whole host of both broad and narrow definitions. Myself, many others, and at least one major dictionary, now simply use the term to refer to 'sourcing' things from the 'crowd', with mass collaborative web tools employed to prevent too many cooks from spoiling the broth.[87]

Others argue that crowdsourcing is solely concerned with bringing the 'crowd' into 'outsourcing' arrangements, and hence only refers to situations where a work activity is advertised and allocated through an online public tender or 'open call'. Although some still cling to this narrow definition, increasingly they are in the minority. I therefore make no apology herein for using the 'crowdsourcing' term to refer to all situations that involve mass online collaboration.

A WINDOWSILL COMMUNITY

Like many new things, crowdsourcing is best understood by example. To this end, in some previous chapters I have already signalled how crowdsourcing is starting to take hold. For instance, back in the first chapter I described an online community called Windowfarms. This is developing home-made, vertical hydroponic gardens to grow food in people's windows. In the process, the Windowfarms community allows ordinary citizens to help solve environmental problems.

Windowfarms was started by 'research and develop-it-yourself' (R&D-I-Y) enthusiast Britta Riley, who built the first Windowfarm in her fifth-floor Brooklyn apartment in 2008. With the prototype complete and the goal set of harvesting a salad a week from an average window, Rita shared her initial designs on a social media website. Within months, people around the world – from Italy to Finland, and Hong Kong to Spain – started to build their own Windowfarms. Through their mass online collaboration, problems were identified, solutions proposed and tested, and new techniques shared for building the best systems and growing different kinds of plants.

The whole premise of Windowfarms is that everybody in its community can contribute small innovations, and that in aggregate these result in highly effective, ever-evolving designs that are tailored to the climate and materials available in different countries. To this end, the initiative has proved very successful, with over 36,000 people now participating in the online community at our.Windowfarms.org.[88]

As Britta Riley argues, with each contribution made it is easier for the next person who joins to build their own Windowfarm. As she further explains, what has been created is 'a multi-disciplinary team of hackers, foodies, teachers [and] gardeners' who collaborate online, all around the world, to help solve 'the environmental problem of how to supply fresh, local food to people in cities'.[89]

OPEN SOURCE SOLUTIONS

The Windowfarms Project is a fantastic example of crowd-sourcing in action. But it is far from the only such venture. In fact, ever since the early days of the public Internet, groups of enthusiasts have recognized the planetary network's potential as a platform for mass collaboration and new product development.

Today, the popular face of crowdsourcing is epitomized by two pioneering communities that use the web to create and distribute free software. One of these is responsible for the OpenOffice software suite, while the other has developed the Linux operating system. Each of these communities creates computer program source code that is freely shared online, and which may be used by anybody under appropriate public licences. Any initiative in which the involved intellectual property is freely distributed is therefore now referred to as 'open source'.

The OpenOffice suite is a free word processor, spreadsheet, presentations and drawing package available from openoffice.org. From the start the goal was 'to create, as a community, the leading international office suite that will run on all major platforms'.[90] Work started in October 2000, with the first version of OpenOffice launched on 30th April 2002. Since the project began, tens of thousands of people – from unaffiliated individuals and students, to business and government employees – have worked to create 'the best possible office suite that all can use'.[91] As a result of their labours, OpenOffice is now available for all major computer operating systems (including Windows and Mac OS). It also supports over 100 languages, and has been freely downloaded over 300 million times.[92]

While OpenOffice provides the world with a free word processor and spreadsheet, the Linux community develops its own operating system as an alternative to Windows or Mac OS. Linux started life as a basic kernel of code freely shared with the world by programmer Linus Torvalds in 1991. Since that time, Linux has been developed by its user community to become a leading operating system that is used on servers, desktop PCs, mobile phones, televisions and the majority of the world's fastest supercomputers.

Linux now comes in many different variants known as 'distributions'. Each of these is based on a common base code, but has been tailored for a specific purpose. While most Linux distributions are free for anybody to download and install, some large corporations sell their own. In return they contribute to Linux development, with the intellectual property they create becoming freely available to the wider Linux community. Linux therefore provides an interesting example of how traditional businesses can successfully engage in crowdsourced undertakings. In fact, a recent analysis of the Linux code kernel revealed that about 75 per cent of it has now been developed by programmers employed by businesses, rather than enthusiast volunteers.[93]

To ensure that Linux does not become a commercial product, since 2000 its growth has been fostered by a non-profit consortium called the Linux Foundation. This 'promotes, protects and advances Linux by marshalling the resources of its members and the open source development community to ensure Linux remains free and technically advanced'.[94]

OPEN DESIGN TAKES HOLD
From producing food in windows, to computer software development and beyond, the practice of 'open design' is now growing rapidly. As argued in the book *Open Design Now* – itself a collaborative undertaking – design is undergoing a revolution. As the authors claim, 'technology is empowering more people to create and disseminate designs, and professionals and enthusiasts are using it to share their work with the world'.[95] Open design is therefore starting to change everything from how things are made to how designers earn a living.

An example of open design's amazing potential is demonstrated by RepRap. This is an open source community that develops and publishes specifications for personal 3D printers. Their crowdsourced designs are called RepRaps – or 'replicating rapid-prototypers' – because they are capable of printing out many of the components required to build another. As RepRep.org explains:

> . . . RepRap takes the form of a free desktop 3D printer capable of printing plastic objects. Since many parts of RepRap are made from plastic and RepRap prints those parts, RepRap self-replicates by making a kit of itself – a kit that anyone can assemble given time and materials. It also means that – if you've got a RepRap – you can print lots of useful stuff, and you can print another RepRap for a friend.[96]

RepRap was founded in 2005 by Adrian Bowyer from the University of Bath, and was the first project to help people build a 3D printer for a few hundred dollars. Hot on its heels in 2006, a similar initiative called Fab@Home was started at Cornell University by Hod Lipson and Evan Malone. A now equally thriving community, this has the impressive goal 'to facilitate the democratization of innovation by giving each household the ability to physically create their ideas'.[97] As the project's website at fabathome.org further explains:

> Fab@Home will change the way we live. It is a platform of printers and programs which can produce functional 3D objects. It is designed to fit on your desktop and within your budget. Fab@Home is supported by a global, open-source community of professionals and hobbyists, innovating tomorrow, today. Join us, and Make Anything.[98]

Other open source communities with great and noble ambitions include those with the intention of creating greener forms of transport. For example, over at theoscarproject.org there is a community developing an open source car or 'OScar'. The idea is that a community of people will plan and develop a new car on the web, and in doing so further convey the potential of crowdsourced open design. Indeed, OScar's champions very much want it to be 'a precursor for many different projects in this field'.[99]

While OScar is still in its early stages, the Riversimple Open Source Hydrogen Car Project has already produced a prototype vehicle. Called the Hyrban, this two-seater, carbon-framed car has already been driven, with a 30-vehicle, year-long pilot of their public use taking place in the English counties of Herefordshire and Shropshire across 2012 and 2013. Riversimple is also one of the most interesting examples to date of a business embracing an open source philosophy.

As the company espouses, its aim is to produce highly energy-efficient vehicles for personal transport using open source design and development.[100] This means that designers and engineers from around the world are helping to develop the vehicle design, with any manufacturer free to produce them. The intention is to make vehicles in small-scale distributed facilities. This will be possible because the economies of scale of carbon composite frames are very different from those of steel-bodied vehicles. Riversimple therefore believes that its vehicles are likely to be built in small factories each producing about 5,000 vehicles per year.[101] The Riversimple approach is therefore highly compatible with the future necessity for more local manufacturing.

To facilitate its novel philosophy, Riversimple has set up a not-for-profit company called the 40 Fires Foundation to which it has licensed its designs. The Foundation's website at 40Fires.org contains an invitation 'to the world's engineers, tinkerers, inventors and vehicle enthusiasts to help . . . develop a sustainable car the open source way'.[102] Entrepreneurs around the world are able to download drawings and data from the site, so allowing them to develop and build their own versions of the Hyrban for their local market.

Other open source initiatives based around the crowd-sourcing model include the Open Prosthetics Project at openprosthetics.org. This is a collaboration between users, designers and funding bodies that works to produce and rapidly share useful innovations in the field of prosthetics.[103] There are also many communities working on the development of open source robots, including the Open Source Robotics Foundation (osrfoundation.org), the Leaf Project (leafproject.org), and the Open Source Micro-robotic Project (swarmrobot.org).

THE RIGHT SIDE OF THE CURVE

By now you are hopefully getting the idea that many different online communities are starting to develop innovative products in a completely new, open and mass collaborative way. Windowfarms, OpenOffice, Linux, RepRap, Fab@ Home, OScar, Riversimple, the Open Prosthetics Project, and the Open Source Robotics Foundation, may all be very different undertakings. But what they have in common is the harnessing of collective online talent to engage in the development of something likely to be viewed as too long-term, complex or otherwise risky to attract mainstream business resources.

One could argue that most open source developers are idealists intent on changing the world in the name of the public good. This may even be true. Yet in the face of those grand challenges on the near horizon, any community that embraces a post-short-term-economic approach to new product development is almost certainly on the right side of the curve.

Others attempting to get otherwise impossible projects off the ground using a crowdsourcing approach have pioneered a related practice known as crowdfunding. Here, rather than pooling their intelligence online, contributors pool their money to help something they believe in get created.

For example, when Brook Drumm in Lincoln, California wanted to create a new, low-cost 3D printer called Printrbot, he needed to raise some funds. He did this by creating a project on Kickstarter.com. Brook's funding target was $25,000, which people could contribute to by pledging any amount of money from $1 to over $999. For $1, contributors would be listed on the Printrbot.com website as 'supporters', while for $10 they would receive a 3D printed bottle opener, and for $199 they would get a bare-bones Printrbot kit. For $499 contributors would be sent a full kit, for $750 an assembled and calibrated Printrbot, and for $999 an assembled, calibrated 3D printer in a hand-painted wooden box.

Like all Kickstarter projects, Printrbot was set up with a fixed closing date, and had to receive pledges at least equal to the full funding requirement before any money changed hands. In the end, $830,828 was pledged against the $25,000 funding target. Printrbot is therefore now a reality, with the business and its website thriving online.

Not all projects submitted to Kickstarter get accepted by the site, and not all of these reach their funding target. Even so, in 2011 Kickstarter raised over $100 million for crowd-funded projects. The projects that get funded are also, by definition, those most likely to find a market. Once again, the power of the crowd has a hand in guiding those innovations that take off.

Inevitably Kickstarter has several competitors. These include Crowdfunder (crowdfunder.co.uk) and Crowdcube (crowdcube.com). The latter is an equity-based crowdfunding platform that 'gives the UK's entrepreneurs and business pioneers a new way to raise business finance by tapping into a "crowd" of like-minded individuals willing to invest smaller amounts of cash in exchange for rewards and a stake in their business'.[104] As yet another take on the concept, at unbound. co.uk authors can crowdfund their writing by pitching book ideas to potential readers. Those readers who back a book before it reaches its funding target then get their names printed in the back of every copy.

WORKING IN NEW WAYS

As I mentioned near the start of this chapter, crowdsourcing can facilitate a new mode of online outsourcing. For example, via the graphic design website crowdSPRING.com, clients requiring a new logo can put out an 'open call' to its community of designers. Many creative people then contribute their ideas – the average being about 110 per project[105] – and the client selects and engages the designer they most favour. Similar services are offered by 99designs.co.uk and Genius-Rocket.com.

Taking a slightly different approach, Amazon Mechanical Turk (AMT) provides a 'marketplace for work that requires human intelligence'.[106] Anybody with a computer and Internet access can register on the site. This on-demand, online workforce can then be called on by organizations who want to build human intelligence directly into their online systems. Or as Amazon explain:

> While computing technology continues to improve, there are still many things that human beings can do much more effectively than computers, such as identifying objects in a

photo or video, performing data de-duplication, transcribing audio recordings or researching data details. Traditionally, tasks like this have been accomplished by hiring a large temporary workforce (which is time consuming, expensive and difficult to scale) or have gone undone.

Mechanical Turk aims to make accessing human intelligence simple, scalable, and cost-effective. Businesses or developers needing tasks done (called Human Intelligence Tasks or 'HITs') can use the robust Mechanical Turk APIs to access thousands of high quality, low cost, global, on-demand workers – and then programmatically integrate the results of that work directly into their business processes and systems.[107]

Several of my students have registered on Amazon Mechanical Turk to gain first-hand experience of the system and the kind of work it allocates. One of them was given the task of finding out if certain hotels were dog-friendly. A list of hotel web addresses was provided, with the instruction to visit each of them to find out if dogs were allowed. Payment was then made according to the number of websites surveyed.

In effect, Amazon Mechanical Turk in particular, and sites like crowdSPRING more generally, allow anybody to telework from anywhere without having to find an employer who offers this option. The downside is clearly that people may be exploited, with those answering open calls in a competitive environment often putting in a great deal of time for no reward whatsoever. On the upside, at least the opportunity now exists to do paid digital work from any location in any country. Organizations with big ideas that they want to rapidly deploy can also put together an online workforce very quickly indeed. In the near-future, post Peak Oil world in which far fewer people will be able to travel, crowdsourced workstyles may also become an important aspect of a new, less resource-intensive mode of globalization.

THE POWER OF VIRTUAL COMMUNITY

In their best-selling book *Abundance*, Peter Diamandis and Steven Kotler passionately argue that cooperative online tools are now reshaping our globe and empowering individuals to step up to the plate and change the world.[108] As we have seen, such tools are already allowing open source communities to innovate new products, as well as permitting some people to work in new ways. In addition, we should also not ignore the growing opportunities for online communities to provide practical and emotional support at the level of the individual.

Human beings have always had a strong desire to communicate and share. Long ago, our ancestors posted their stories on the walls of caves. Today, the Internet has become the cave wall of the modern age. However, rather than being a static, stone medium, its digital wall is something we can all write on – and share on – for the interactive, common good. In the past people built physical walls to keep others out. And yet today, on Facebook, YouTube and Twitter – and across a myriad of other online lairs – we build virtual walls to allow others into our souls.

Contrary to what many non- or occasional users appreciate, the Internet is basically people. Teenagers sitting alone at a computer or smartphone are usually far more addicted to digital human interaction than silicon, plastic and code. Across the world, human beings are starting to collectively share their lives as never before. But this is still a dark secret to which many remain blind.

Last summer I underwent hernia surgery. Fortunately it was not a medical emergency, and so a prior consultation with my surgeon gave me some idea of what to expect.

Nevertheless, like many people in my situation, I also researched what the operation would be like by drawing on the social media contributions of strangers.

In particular I watched some YouTube videos made by two young men in the United States who had undergone exactly the same surgery. In heartfelt video diaries recorded immediately before and after their operations, I saw their fear and heard their outcomes. Not that long ago I was also faced with the prospect of a bone marrow biopsy. For a second time I therefore watched videos on YouTube to learn what to expect. Once again these were not official hospital guides, but raw footage from real patients (or their loved ones) who had picked up their smartphones to share their experiences both inside and outside the operating room.

Medicine – like politics – is no longer a closed game. Many non-users may still think that the Internet is about computing. But it really is not. It is about people linking to people, often in known groups or relationships, but frequently also sharing with the crowd for the common good.

Another stark example of the power of social media was brought to the attention of millions in the United Kingdom in August 2011. During this month, rioting occurred in many major cities. In part there was some organization behind these disturbances, with rioters and looters sharing their plans on Twitter and Facebook. The potentially dangerous aspects of mass online collaboration were therefore revealed.

On the positive side, social media played an important role in helping many to deal with the riots. For example, in my own city of Nottingham, the police used the Twitter hashtag '#NottsPoliceLatest' to provide a running information service as five police stations and two schools were firebombed. Hundreds also supported the police on Twitter – thanking them for their actions, passing on incident information, and planning clean-up teams. Using Twitter, the police were very quickly able to quash false reports and rumours. As Assistant Chief Constable Paul Broadbent argued, while during this troubled time social media helped rioters and looters, they also spread positive messages quickly. By monitoring online sources minute-by-minute, crowdsourcing tools also helped the police to respond most effectively to keep the public safe.[109]

Without doubt, social media is the phenomenon of the moment. The fact that Facebook now has more members than any country has citizens – and that many people's response in times of jubilation or crisis is to seek out others on the Internet – indeed has to say something about the way our civilization is evolving. For most of human history, communities were based around groups of people who lived in the same place. But today, online tools are increasingly allowing people to affiliate with 'virtual communities of interest' that coalesce on demand in cyberspace.

Some virtual communities – such as circles of Facebook friends or Twitter followers – are often comprised of people who know each other by name and who sometimes meet in person. In contrast, most virtual communities of interest are powerful yet individually transient. From the perspective of their 'users', they spring into existence only when a mutual interest is momentarily shared in the same medical condition, social problem, product, or anything else that has garnered mental traction. Such virtual communities are largely created and sustained by crowdsourcing contributions made by strangers for strangers. Yet somehow this rarely diminishes their value. The video diary of an unknown patient, the review on Amazon of an amazing new gadget, or the blog about removing a stubborn stain, still usually prove of personal and even emotional significance whether or not we know their creators.

As John Michael Greer argues in *The Long Descent*, community – rather than the isolated individual – is the basic unit of human survival. It is therefore a great pity that the Petroleum Age has seen the twilight of community across the industrialized world in favour of a mass society knitted together almost entirely by global economic exchange.[110] This perhaps explains why hundreds of millions of people are reaching out to establish community connections online, with many prepared to invest heavily in the creation of online content with no apparent personal reward.

For some, there is now more of a 'home' to be found online than in the geographic area in which they physically live. Many may argue this to be terribly sad and a really bad thing. Yet it is surely more important that people find solace and support somewhere. We should also not forget that, once people learn to contribute to mass activities online, significant benefits may accrue for us all. To help fix the world, the trend for mass online information exchange and collaboration is something that needs to be embraced rather than feared.

BIG DATA

All of the crowdsourcing developments outlined so far require people to make conscious online contributions. For example, open source communities rely on members prepared to submit, discuss or test innovations, while those sharing their experiences on YouTube have to make and upload videos. There are, however, also increasing possibilities to develop a new mode of crowdsourcing that can generate value from our largely unconscious digital footprints.

'Big Data' is the new kid on the computing block, and refers to the processing of very large quantities of digital information that cannot be analyzed with traditional computing techniques. For many years, some retailers have tried to monitor their customers using point-of-sale loyalty cards. In this pursuit, a few – including Walmart in the United States and Tesco in the United Kingdom – have successfully managed to improve their market position. Even so, the technology has not existed to mine more than a small percentage of the data collected. The vast majority of the information captured via retailer loyalty cards has therefore been discarded as 'data exhaust'.

Because loyalty cards provide a record of every single customer transaction, the quantity of data they can generate is vast. The digital trails – or 'data shadows' – now being left by most Internet users as they surf, shop and communicate are also creating tremendous quantities of data. In addition, an incredible volume of digital output is today being generated by digital cameras, tracking sensors, medical scanners, and mind-bogglingly-complex scientific research in areas including nanotechnology, nuclear fusion and synthetic biology.

In response, new data processing technologies are starting to be created. These are able to capture and analyze the Big Data sets that traditional computing techniques simply cannot handle. Already this is starting to create new business opportunities that large companies are keen to exploit and of which it may be easy to disapprove. Yet before we start to protest too strongly about the dangers of Big Data, we need to recognize the potential it presents to save energy and other resources.

Today, organizations large and small have to try and predict what resources need to be allocated where and why. Products get made in the hope that people may want them. Meanwhile hospitals are built, surgical supplies are manufactured, and medical staff are trained, in the expectation of certain levels of illness in particular locations. In fact, pretty much all of the planning on which the fluid functioning of our civilization depends is based on no more than informed guesswork. But crowdsourced Big Data could change all that.

For example, hospitals have a very high level of data exhaust. Not least, the video data that is recorded in keyhole surgery and similar procedures is typically deleted within weeks or even days. Clearly this may be detrimental to individual patients if they develop longer-term complications. But it is also a cruel loss for wider society. Imagine if a Big Data system with powerful vision recognition capabilities was set to work analyzing and cross-correlating all of the medical imagery and test results captured and otherwise recorded in every hospital on every single day. Such a system would be able to spot developing trends in the health of the population that no human doctor or health service manager could ever hope to detect. The utilization of healthcare resources could subsequently be significantly improved, with waste kept to an absolute minimum.

The above scenario may sound like a future fantasy. But already there are artificial intelligence systems that can process scan data and patient histories to diagnose cancer more reliably than a human doctor. It should also be noted that a 2011 McKinsey Global Institute report estimated that Big Data could deliver $300 billion in efficiency and quality savings every year in the US healthcare sector alone.[111] This would be the equivalent of an 8 per cent cost reduction across the board, and illustrates how the potential to use Big Data to help save resources is very real.

The same McKinsey report estimated that, across the European Union, Big Data could be used to save at least $149 billion in government administration costs annually.[112] More broadly, in manufacturing firms, integrating Big Data across R&D, engineering and production may significantly reduce time to market, improve product quality, and decrease materials wastage. Recognizing the potential, in May 2012 the US government announced an investment of $200 million in Big Data projects.[113]

Big Data potentially has a vast number of applications. For example, it could be employed to help save energy and reduce greenhouse gas emissions by improving traffic management in cities, as well as permitting the smarter operation of electricity generation infrastructures. In time, Big Data climate simulation models may even allow farmers to accurately forecast bad weather and crop failures. And governments may use Big Data to predict and plan for civil unrest.

The potential mass processing of everybody's data shadows could develop into a very significant resource allocation tool (although admittedly it could also be subverted into a mass surveillance mechanism). Unfortunately at present, while new Big Data software technologies are being developed – the most prominent being called Hadoop – the processing power required for planetary-scale Big Data analysis does not exist. But in as little as a decade the situation could be very different. Recent developments in the fledgling science of quantum computing suggest that extraordinarily powerful pattern-matching and artificial intelligence systems may be with us sooner rather than later. In fact, the first commercial quantum computer – the D-Wave One from Canada's D-Wave Systems – was sold to Lockheed Martin in May 2011.

Even before next-generation quantum computers arrive, many governments have recognized the potential to share very large datasets for the public good. For example, the UK government has already released nearly 9,000 sets of public or 'open data' via its website data.gov.uk. These include health, social care, transport and employment datasets comprised of anonymous, aggregated information unconsciously generated or otherwise supplied by UK citizens. Data is at present the only raw material we can be certain will remain in plentiful supply. We therefore have some incentive to leverage as much value from it as possible in order improve our allocation of scarcer and scarcer physical resources.

A PLANETARY MIND

Kevin Kelly – the co-creator of *Wired* magazine – once argued that 'planetary-scale problems require a planetary-scale mind'.[114] It is therefore somewhat fortunate that, as global challenges continue to accrue, the inorganic systems of the Internet are fast interlinking billions of organic selves. In effect, what all of the different forms of crowdsourcing discussed in this chapter really highlight is how humanity is fast evolving into a collective, global entity in which every human can electronically share with every other.

By trading our thoughts online, we are also starting to develop some very useful tools. Google, for example, has discovered that certain search terms are good indicators of flu activity, and is now aggregating social media data to provide real-time global flu maps. If you are interested - or just planning a trip! – these can be found at google.org/flutrends.

As was witnessed during the Arab Spring, so-termed 'Facebook revolutions' have also become a reality. Activists still need courage to act, but may now at least do so with the knowledge that others share their cause and may act with them or otherwise lend support. No regime has fully learnt how to control or act against social media – although China is having a pretty good stab with the maintenance of the great Internet Firewall that surrounds its nation.

Crowdsourcing has already provided humanity with far more than free computer software, relatively low-cost 3D printers, and new forums for obtaining work. In addition, global knowledge bases like Wikipedia and ifixit.com (a free repair manual that anybody can edit) have been created by the crowd and are already starting to be taken for granted. We now just *expect* the collective knowledge of the human race to be on tap and increasingly on video. What is more, due to mass online contributions, the quality and quantity of information available online is very good indeed.

A few mainstream commercial organizations are also starting to recognize the potential to do things better by in part adopting a crowdsourcing approach. Citroën, for example, has begun to crowdsource car designs on Facebook, with some of the features of its C1 Connexion model chosen by popular vote. As the company explains, it is 'taking the choices of many to create a car for everyone. This is crowdsourcing in action. The New C1 Connexion [is] a car created for the Facebook generation, by the Facebook generation'.[115]

BEYOND BIG BUSINESS

People often ask me how business organizations can make money from the crowdsourcing revolution. As the example of Citroën indicates, opportunities for companies to crowd-source do exist – and I guess by part-designing cars on Facebook, Citroën may sell a few more vehicles. Riversimple may also one day profit from an exploitation of its open source Hyrban designs, while Dell, IBM, HP, Oracle, Novell, Nokia and others will continue to benefit from their close association with the Linux development community. These cases noted, I would caution that crowdsourcing and profit generation may frequently turn out to be incompatible.

As crowdsourcing gathers momentum, we may well be entering a world in which an increasing proportion of productive activity will no longer involve business and the monetary economy. With the rise of the Internet, there really is no reason that for-profit organizations and financial exchange have to continue to dominate the way we create things and share them with our fellow human beings. It is indeed perfectly possible that, rather than continuing to allow for-profit organizations to make everything we consume, we may in the future choose to help each other out a bit more without a business bottom line getting in the way.

Today, if you own a computer, there is often no reason to install a commercial operating system or a commercial office suite. This is because, over the past decade, Linux and OpenOffice have managed to get such a foothold in personal computing that many people and many businesses are now more than happy to rely on their open-source, crowd-sourced software. YouTube and Wikipedia's vast hoard of free, crowdsourced media content is also something that many now take for granted. As initiatives like RepRap, Fab@Home and Windowfarms become more established, we are also likely to welcome even more free things into our lives. These will be at least part-crowdsourced into exist-ence by the collective efforts of talented enthusiasts, rather than designed, manufactured and mass-marketed by faceless corporations that demand money every time they supply anything to us.

I am not here advocating the end of the whole capitalist system as we know it (although I will chip away at it a little more in chapter 7!). This said, it is possible that crowdsourcing will cause the Internet to evolve beyond communication and media exchange, and into a planetary platform for product innovation and free service delivery. In ten years, it is perfectly possible that most of the computer software, literature, video, education and training that most people require will be created via crowdsourcing and delivered via the web. A great deal of medical advice – not to mention help with growing a bit of your own food and producing some of your own energy – could also be freely available online.

While valuable, none of the above services will feature in any of those measures of gross domestic product (GDP) that mainstream economists, journalists and politicians continue to obsess about. This really should not matter, although it may confuse economists if economies start to shrink while standards of welfare rise. In this context, the really big implication of crowdsourcing for businesses to get their corporate heads around is that people may start to do without them a little bit as we all learn to look after each other rather than the economy. Or in other words, the ultimate impact of crowdsourcing may be that we will not need or want for-profit organizations in our lives quite as much as we collectively demand them today.

* * *

COMMUNITY OVER COMPETITION

As you may by now have gathered, I have quite a few pet hates. Close to the top of my list are TV news reporters and other journalists who have made it their unelected mission to destructively and often rudely criticize everything and everybody. In the United Kingdom, such characters are epitomized by the likes of the BBC's Jeremy Paxman and Channel 4's Jon Snow. While both are respected newscasters of great stature, neither seems capable of conducting an interview that is anything other than hypercritical. Both have been weaned on a competition culture that celebrates the reporting of failure and disaster, and which demands them to seek out the negative even when it does not exist. If you live in the United Kingdom you will probably be familiar with these guys. And if not – and you live in a relatively free society – you will know people like them from your own telly screens.

Of course, it is not just acerbic newscasters who dedicate their existence to constant argument and negativity. For a start, many democratic systems allow their citizens to vote one party into power, and then immediately label another the official 'opposition' with a remit to denigrate every little thing that the Government does. As a consequence, politics worldwide has descended into a petty and aggressive competition, with point-scoring rather than substance dominating almost all political debate. This is not just fruitless, but also rather sad given that most mainstream politicians agree on many of the problems to be addressed, and sometimes even on a few of the solutions. Although anybody who follows politics solely via the 24 hour media would not necessarily know this.

As I stated at the start of this chapter, cooperation beats competition. As I also hope to have shown, the use of the Internet as a crowdsourcing platform now offers fresh possibilities for people to work together in new ways. It is therefore very disappointing that most journalists, economists and politicians still try their best to champion competition over cooperation.

What we need are more people in charge of organizations and governments who are inclined to put community first. It is potentially therefore fortunate that, in very broad terms, about half of our species are genetically predisposed to harbour such a characteristic. The next chapter therefore sets out our future requirement to have far more women in authority.

6

MORE WOMEN IN AUTHORITY

For many years futurists have been predicting the future to be female. This is based on an expectation that social and community-building skills will increasingly triumph over brute force and outright competition. As futurist Ian Pearson argues, a new 'care economy' is emerging in which people will have to focus far more on their emotional skills, and women are instinctively better at this than men.[116] Or as Daniel Burrus, the bestselling author of *Flash Foresight*, explains, 'the number one certainty is that the future is all about relationships' and 'this is where women shine'.[117]

Making broad generalizations about women and men is a precarious activity for any author. I therefore want to acknowledge from the outset that everybody is an individual, with few if any of us appropriately characterized by a mass sexual stereotype. Nevertheless, it is blatantly obvious that women and men are psychologically wired somewhat differently, and that this in general results in the two sexes having somewhat different qualities as leaders, employees and community members.

My argument in this chapter is that, to fix the world, we need to have far more women in authority at all levels and in all types of organization. I am not going to suggest that the world should be run by women. But neither is it sensible for things to continue to be run almost entirely by men. Given that we are born in almost equal measure, the optimal mix of females to males in positions of authority ought in most instances to be about 50:50.

By forging male-dominated power structures, the human race has done much to sew the potential seeds of its own downfall. Indeed, our civilization arguably now faces some of its most difficult decades precisely because we have for far too long failed to incorporate an appropriate female perspective into our key decision making mechanisms.

To fix the world, we need to start forging more caring and sharing community structures that are capable of putting the long-term survival of the majority ahead of short-term individual greed. Almost certainly, this will not happen without both women and men in authority in equal measure. It is therefore now time for us all to appreciate that female and male perspectives are highly complementary, with no species able to excel without drawing equally on the strength of both sexes.

TESTOSTERONE IN THE CITY

In 2007 and 2008, the meltdown of the global financial system almost brought the world to ruin. Much of what happened was an inevitable consequence of several decades of reckless borrowing and the rise of mass consumerism. Yet, as in any crisis, there were inevitably particular pressure points and signature calamity events. In the United Kingdom, the first of these was the fall of Northern Rock in September 2007, followed by the collapse of the Royal Bank of Scotland the following November. Across the Atlantic, the most significant events occurred in September 2008 with the federal takeovers of Fannie Mae and Freddie Mac, swiftly followed by the bankruptcy of Lehman Brothers.

Since the world's banking system almost went completely bust, many authors have provided their take on the cancerous City culture that cost so many so much. One of the most interesting is *Confessions of a City Girl* by Barbara Stcherbatcheff.[118] This tells the tale of her fight to escape a backroom office job and to become a City trader. In this quest Barbara was repeatedly told that 'trading is no job for a girl', with women having 'to work ten times harder and be ten times smarter than the guys'. Then as now, only 7 per cent of front office employees in many City institutions were female, with women having 'more chance of becoming an astronaut or Michelin-starred chef than a top hedge fund manager'.

Against the odds, Barbara did make it in a male-dominated world – if only to find that 'there appeared to be an entirely different pay scale for men and women's bonuses'. During her time on the trading floor, Barbara worked with male traders who exhibited an intensely rude and aggressive 'macho herd mentality', and whose attitude to taking risks was cavalier. Those back-office analysts who even dared to suggest that traders ought to be more prudent were ignored, or else mocked, humiliated and pushed back to the sidelines.

As the financial crisis of 2007 and 2008 got worse and worse, Barbara concluded that while men thought they ruled the world, their fiercely-competitive behaviour was actually screwing it up. As she wrote, 'I swear guys will make the same mistake again and again just so that, by the law of averages, one day they can say "I won". [But] the cost of this egotistical obsession is extremely high'.[119] It is therefore perhaps not a surprise that, across the City, it was men who were involved in most of the frauds and scandals, while a lot of the whistleblowers were women.

In the wake of the downturn, Barbara came to believe that the whole credit crunch could have been avoided if there had been more women in the City. This might seem a bizarre and biased conclusion. Yet today, the view that testosterone-fuelled thinking was the cause of so much darn-right-scandalous risk taking is being seriously entertained in many quarters. For example, as a leading financial website mused in 2009:

> Would [women] have been more focused on the human consequences and less on the next pay cheque? Would they have been more empathetic and less cut-throat? Would financial districts have had a few more crèches and a few less of those godawful bars where traders hang out to brag about their latest deal? In short, would we have avoided this calamity if markets had been doused with sufficient quantities of oestrogen?[120]

For some, the answer to the above question is a most emphatic 'yes'. As the highly successful Norwegian investor and businesswoman Anna Cecilie Holst once sought to explain:

> Women are more afraid than men. And this can be both positive and negative. In the financial world, I think it is positive. Women are not risk-driven. Men are competitive, they like to take risks. Basically by nature, women are more risk averse. I don't think Lehman Sisters would have taken the same risks as Lehman Brothers. Women are used to managing budgets at home. We know what a balanced budget means. We think ahead, we are not driven by the same ego. We have to plan, we are protective. Some of this crisis was based on greed and individuals showing off about how much they were earning. Women don't have the need to promote themselves in this way. We understand the meaning of financial management.[121]

Anna is not the only top financial businesswoman to believe that women are likely to behave in a more risk-averse and less materialistic way than men. For example, the same view is held by the Swiss banker and co-founder of Axia Investments Anne Hornung-Soukup. As Anne highlights in her own analysis of the financial crisis:

> All those who made huge bonuses while driving their institutions into financial ruin were men. Fannie Mae and Freddie Mac were headed by men as they went overboard giving mortgages to low income people who didn't know any better. UBS was headed by men as it launched itself into derivatives way beyond its capacity for risk control. AIG in the US, Northern Rock in the UK, HypoBank in Germany, all were headed by men.[122]

As Anne argues, there is hard evidence that women are better credit risks as clients, more prudent as investors and managers, and likely to take more cautious decisions as regulators. To cite an absolutely critical example, in 1997 Brooksley Born – the former female Chair of the Commodities Futures Trading Association in the US – asked Congress to tighten the regulation of the derivatives market in order to prevent a possible crisis. This call and warning were resisted and then ignored by her male colleagues, with disastrous consequences that the whole world continues to suffer. In this context, it is also interesting to note that, before 2009, the central banks of all European Union member states had a male governor, with their key decision-making bodies having a male-to-female ratio of 82-to-18.[123]

Anne Hornung-Soukup also points out that, following the collapse of its banking system, the Icelandic government turned to women to change its banking culture. To achieve this, female executives Elín Sigfúsdóttir and Birna Einarsdóttir were appointed to run the nationalized banks New Landisbank and New Glitnir. As Anne explains:

> The problems in Iceland [are] believed to have been created largely by aggressive young and not-so-young males, egged on by generous short-term bonus plans, who proceeded to load up their institutions' balance sheets with incredibly excessive foreign debt. This risk-taking behaviour, which led the banks, and the entire country, straight into a brick wall, [has been] changed by the new female CEOs to one of conservatism and prudent lending.[124]

Much of the above analysis could potentially be dismissed as biased speculation based on a stereotypical perception of males. It is therefore worth noting that, in 2010, the European Commission published a detailed report that highlighted how the 'lack of women in economic decision making positions in Europe' was an impediment to 'economic stability and growth'.[125]

In November 2008, a study from Harvard even demonstrated that men with higher levels of testosterone took more risks when placing financial bets. For example, a 33 per cent higher testosterone level resulted in the placing of 10 per cent riskier bets.[126]

Levels of testosterone are known to rise when men are placed in competitive situations. High testosterone levels may also be perpetuated in male-dominated workplaces such as financial trading floors. As Anna Dreber, one of the authors of the Harvard study, subsequently concluded in an interview, 'long-term, above-average testosterone levels may perhaps eventually lead to irrational risk-taking'.[127]

What the Harvard study absolutely demonstrated is that the more testosterone is involved in a trade, the riskier it is likely to be, and the more likely it is to fail to earn a profit.

Given that financial institutions actively seek out the most competitive and hence testosterone-charged men to do their trading, the Harvard study ought subsequently to provide much food for thought. Backing it up, other research has shown that male investors really do lose money more often than female traders, even though men still believe that they are better investors than women.[128] In fact, according to a 2008 study of the testosterone levels in London traders, 'long periods of elevated testosterone, as might be the case during a market bubble, [can even] turn risk-taking into a form of addiction'.[129]

As all of these studies suggest, a strong female perspective would be highly likely to reduce excessive risk taking on the financial markets. With more women on trading floors and in other senior positions in the City, the banks and other financial institutions on which we all depend would therefore be more secure. It is hence a great pity that, as Barbara Stcherbatcheff discovered, 'the city is threatened by women' and does its best to keep them out, even if its performance suffers dangerously as a result. Or as one of the few senior female bankers who advised Barbara put it, 'even if you do break through the glass ceiling, you'll still be expected to pick up the glass'.[130]

BOOSTING THE BOTTOM LINE

It is not just in the dangerous fantasy lands of the financial markets that things could be improved by putting more women in charge. As argued by 'womenomics' champions 20-First.com, appointing more women to positions of authority is 'a business issue, not a women's issue'. This is because 'women now represent a majority of the talent pool, [and] a majority of the market', with a better gender balance in organizations even 'yielding better corporate perfor- mance'.[131] While these assertions from 20-First may sound like particularly zealous claims, they are surprisingly easy to validate.

When it comes to education, globally the number of women obtaining a degree is now higher than the number of men. In fact, across Europe and the United States, 60 per cent of new graduates are currently female.[132] As a direct consequence, 53 per cent of entry-level professional employees in the United States are women.[133] Organizations therefore have a significant female talent pool to pick from when choosing their future middle and senior managers. In fact, if future employment patterns were based purely on educational attainment, within a few decades the majority of middle and senior managers would be women.

In terms of market power, while women are underrepresented in most organizational decision making structures, they have for decades directed the majority of domestic spending. For example, in a family involving a mixed-sex couple, women make 92 per cent of vacation decisions, 91 per cent of home purchase decisions, 80 per cent of healthcare decisions, and 60 per cent of the decisions related to obtaining a new family car. As Daniel Burrus subsequently concludes, 'women are not just influencing the market; they *are* the market'.[134] It is therefore somewhat bizarre that most organizations are not chaffing at the bit to employ more female managers and executives in order to get closer to their key customer base.

There is also very serious evidence that placing more women in authority is likely to have a positive impact on the corporate bottom line – and not just when it comes to stock market trading. For example, a few years ago, management consultants McKinsey & Company conducted a study of 89 top European companies to assess the impact of women board members on organizational performance. Between 2005 and 2007, their findings proved with 'no doubt' that companies with a higher proportion of women on their boards outperformed others in the same sector. Specifically, both a higher return on equity and a stronger stock market growth were achieved in companies with more female board members.[135]

A similar study, conducted by Catalyst in the United States, found that the Fortune 500 companies with the highest ratio of female board directors strongly outperformed those with the fewest women included. The figures here were in fact quite breathtaking, with companies with the highest ratio of women on the board achieving a 42 per cent higher return on sales and a 66 per cent higher return on capital invested.[136]

Meanwhile in the United Kingdom, firms with at least one female board member have been found to be 20 per cent less likely to go bust, with those having more than one female board member even less likely to fail.[137] Over in Australia, Goldman Sachs has calculated that closing the female-male employment gap to make optimal use of the country's available talent could boost the level of Australian GDP by 11 per cent.[138]

THE STRUGGLE FOR EQUALITY

Despite the paybacks highlighted in the previous section, the potential contributions of women to our ailing civilization remain seriously undervalued. Many women today do have more rights than their female ancestors of a century ago. But even so, there is still far from a level playing field. It is also worth reminding ourselves just how recent even today's level of relative female equality actually is.

In the United States, all women only got the right to vote when the Nineteenth Amendment to the Constitution became law on 18th August 1920. In the United Kingdom, the same right came eight years later with the passing of the

Representation of the People (Equal Franchise) Act in 1928. In Switzerland, women only got the right to vote and to stand for parliament in 1971, while in Kuwait this did not occur until 2005. Given that many women alive today were born into democracies in which only men were allowed to participate, it is unfortunately not surprising that women are still greatly underrepresented in most decision making arenas.

Those senior women bankers and businesswomen cited earlier in this chapter sadly remain a rare breed. Indeed, according to the *Grant Thornton International Business Report 2012*, today only 21 per cent of senior managers globally are women. This figure has also remained basically unchanged since 2004.[139]

The proportion of women in positions of authority varies significantly between nations. Russia currently has the highest proportion of women in senior management positions at 46 per cent. This compares to 36 per cent in Italy, 33 per cent in Hong Kong, 28 per cent in South Africa, 25 per cent in China, 20 per cent in the United Kingdom, 17 per cent in the United States, 14 per cent in India, 13 per cent in Germany, and only 5 per cent in Japan. Globally, a quite staggering 34 per cent of companies have no women in senior management positions at all.[140]

In the boardroom, women are even more marginally represented. In the United States, just 3 per cent of Fortune 500 companies are run by women, with only 14 per cent of board members being female. Across the pond in the United Kingdom, women account for just 14.9 per cent of board members in the top 500 FTSE listed companies. In Germany and India, the number of women on executive committees falls to a shameful 2 per cent.[141]

Many reasons have been cited to try and explain this sorry state of affairs. The most common is that women leave the workplace to have children, with this either ending or hindering a top-flight career. While there has to be some logistical truth in this proposition, the biological fact that females bear and care for children simply does not explain why so many women get passed over for promotion long before they start a family, or indeed after their children have grown up. Organizations therefore need to begin asking themselves why they are losing out on so much female talent, and indeed if they can afford to continue doing so.

Almost certainly, the single greatest impediments to the promotion of women are diehard corporate cultures entrenched with legacy male mindsets. In a 2007 survey and report, McKinsey & Company tried to bring these more into the open, with a list of 'mindsets that set up women for failure'.[142]

The first mindset identified was that women are often perceived as either too aggressive or too passive to be given significant responsibility. It was also found that men sometimes feel uncomfortable if they do not promote their male prodigies when a senior position becomes available. In addition to the 'I cannot face telling Bob' syndrome, some men apparently also worry that, if they employ a woman in a senior position, they will not be able to manage or mentor them.

Another common issue is the belief that appointing a woman to a top job could dramatically backfire, with any failure likely to prove a potential setback for all women and not just one employee. Such a view effectively treats only men as individuals, but sadly is not uncommon. Also widespread is the stereotypical belief that some jobs are just not suitable for women. As we have seen, this proposition remains prominent in the City, even though it has been fairly conclusively proven that – over time – women are likely to outperform male traders.

Changing Corporate Minds

If the world is to be fixed, organizations cannot go on ignoring so much female talent. Yet unfortunately, there are no magic bullet solutions. In most countries, the issue is no longer getting women educated and motivated. Rather, what have to change are attitudes and management practices on a wide range of organizational levels.

Perhaps most importantly, both men and women need to appreciate that the last thing that needs to happen is for more women to start 'mastering male codes' and behaving like men.[143] For too long, many of the few women who have risen to the top have achieved their success by developing a harsh, macho persona to help get them noticed and promoted. Such a strategy may have helped Barbara Stcherbatcheff and others to succeed in the male-dominated world of the City. But this tactic will never help to introduce a balancing female perspective into the world's key decision making structures. We need far more women *who behave like women* in authority, rather than females reprogrammed with a male mentality. Mindsets and promotion yardsticks therefore have to change – and both men and women have to take responsibility for this.

In 2007, McKinsey & Company came up with a set of proposals to help 'reshape the talent pipeline' that they observed in most companies. First on their list was the need for organization-wide, top-management buy-in. As they argued, to make the required changes:

> . . . corporate leaders need to see them as no less important than a major strategic or operational challenge, such as falling market share or changing the corporate cost structure. And like efforts to address those challenges, efforts to advance women can't just be add-on programs. They must be integrated into the organization's daily work through goals, perfor-

mance monitoring, processes that force tough conversations, and serious skill building.[144]

Linked to the above, McKinsey proposed that mechanisms need to be introduced to ensure that enough women are shortlisted for senior jobs so that high-talent females are not 'underexposed'. Many organizations remain loath to introduce either candidate or final employment female quotas. Even so, if the male-dominated status quo is to be altered, at the very least informal quotas or high-level formal targets are likely to be necessary to help catalyze change.

Fortunately, some companies are already leading the way. For example, at Time Warner each division is required to put in place robust succession plans and 'promotion slates' for its top layers of management. These are constantly reviewed to ensure that enough women are being prepared for potential promotion to a senior role. This ensures that, when a senior job becomes available, an appropriately balanced shortlist can be constructed.

At Time Warner, executive bonuses are also in part based on the attainment of gender diversity goals. Meanwhile at Shell, a long-term, company-wide target has been set for 20 per cent of senior executives to be female. Already this has had some effect, with the latest figure standing at 15 per cent, compared to 10 per cent in 2005.[145] This example noted, it would of course be better if Shell's target for senior females was 50 per cent.

Related to the setting of quotas and targets, McKinsey also stressed that collecting and transparently sharing data on female employment ratios can prove a powerful tool. As they argued, today many companies have no idea of the ratio of females to males in their talent pipeline – and hence no way to manage or improve its gender balance. In contrast, at a pioneer like PepsiCo, the progress of women at all levels of the business is explicitly monitored and widely communicated. This makes all managers aware when glass ceilings are preventing the promotion or employment of women, so allowing positive action to be taken and mindsets challenged and changed.

As a final proposal, McKinsey suggested that coaching styles often need to be questioned. As they highlight, in many male-dominated organizations, staff are mentored toward possible promotion by 'relentless coaches' who push their best staff almost to breaking point. While many men find this motivational, such an approach does often not work well for women. This is especially the case for those with domestic responsibilities which prevent them from working 70+ hours a week to try and keep even a well-intentioned boss happy.

Similarly, while many men are driven to succeed by a manager who offers little apparent support and constant criticism, many women find this kind of management style a drain on their confidence and highly demotivating.[146] If we are to get more women in authority, diverse management approaches therefore need to be developed that recognize and nurture the different but equally valuable qualities of women and men.

Recognizing the above issues, many governments are now taking measures to try and get more women into senior positions. These range from legislative quotas, to broader regulation, and the announcement of voluntary codes of practice. For example, in 2005 a law was passed in Finland to raise the number of women on boards to 40 per cent. This requires both females and males to be considered in all board-level appointments. In 2007 in Spain, a similar gender equality law was introduced. This mandates companies with more than 250 employees to have at least 40 per cent women on their boards by 2015.

In 2011, France passed a law requiring 40 per cent of board directors in companies with more than 500 employees to be female by 2017. In the same year, Italy and Belgium also enacted legislation that mandates 33 per cent of board directors to be women. Similar laws that set explicit board member quotas have additionally been passed in Iceland, Israel, Kenya, Norway and Quebec. Meanwhile legislation has been proposed in Australia, Canada, the Netherlands and the Philippines.[147]

Somewhat more broadly, 20 countries have now introduced regulations to try and increase female board representation. All of these require companies to disclose their diversity policies, with many also setting targets that companies must either attain, or else formally justify not meeting. The countries concerned include Germany, Iceland, Malaysia, Nigeria, South Africa, Sweden, the United Kingdom and the United States. However, in the United Kingdom requirements are limited to a non-specific corporate governance code, while in the United States there is only a diversity disclosure regulation.

Finally, calls for voluntary initiatives are also spreading. For example, in 2011 the European Union sought a pledge from its members for all publicly listed companies to have at least 30 per cent female board members by 2015, and 40 per cent by 2020. Also in 2011, the UK government announced a voluntary 'target and recommendation' for at least 25 per cent of the boards of FTSE 100 companies to be women by 2015. Meanwhile in the United States, there is now a national '2020 campaign' to increase the percentage of women on all company boards to 20 per cent or greater by 2020.[148]

THE WHOLE GENE POOL

When the final battle is raging on all fronts, a smart general does not leave any of their best troops in the barracks. And yet today, this is exactly the kind of strategy that is being adopted by global humanity. Something clearly has to change, and the governmental measures I have just outlined are at the very least a recognition of this fact.

This point noted, while the laws, regulations and voluntary initiatives described in the previous section are intended as a positive response, they remain controversial and in some countries hotly contested. On the one hand, some men argue that setting quotas and targets for senior female representation discriminates against talented men. Meanwhile, some women argue that they ought to be promoted to senior positions purely on their own merits, rather than 'relying' on legislative or even voluntary 'assistance'.

Those who argue against quotas and targets do potentially have a legitimate point in perfect-world equity terms. But in the real world in which we live, positive discrimination is almost certainly needed for at least a decade to ensure that a more balanced female perspective is rapidly introduced into many key decision making arenas. To misquote 20-First. com, getting far more females into positions of authority is not a women's issue, but a planetary survival issue. And the latter really ought to be our primary concern.

As a report by the UK's Equality and Human Rights Commission highlighted in 2008, unless positive and radical steps are taken, it will take more than 70 years to achieve gender-balanced boardrooms.[149] But unfortunately in 70 or even 25 years time it will be far too late to implement those long-term, community-centric solutions on which the survival of our civilization may well depend, and which females are in general more likely to champion than males.

The ongoing financial crisis really has to serve as a wake-up call. It would simply be suicidal for humanity to let men continue in the majority driving seat as the last of our oil runs dry, the planet heats irrevocably, and food and water shortages kill billions. Targets, quotas and positive discrimination are therefore necessary as a short-term evil regardless of how many well-meaning equity-zealots they may offend. Like any species, to survive and thrive we must capitalize on the life code of our entire gene pool. To do any different would be to ignore so much of the talent that evolution has struggled and fought to encode into female DNA.

Some naysayers may argue that for thousands of years the human race has done just fine by relying on male-dominated decision making structures. To such people I would say just two things. The first is that we may have done even better – and had fewer wars – with more women in authority throughout the ages. Secondly and even more fundamentally, we need to remember that only in the past few centuries has humanity started to make decisions – consciously or otherwise – that have had very long-term, planetary-scale implications. For millennia, any daft human decision had an absolutely minimal influence on the biosphere, and almost no impact on future generations. But today this is no longer the case. We therefore cannot afford to plod and flounder on in a mediocre fashion.

The decisions that humanity collectively takes in the next two decades will have more impact on people tomorrow than at any other time in our history. We therefore owe it to the generations ahead to make the best decisions possible. As both common sense and the evidence presented in this chapter strongly suggest, the best long-term decisions are also likely to be made with women and men standing shoulder-to-shoulder at the helm.

For most of human history, the vast majority of women stayed at home to perform domestic labour while men went off to hunt or fight a war. When physical strength and aggression were used to win battles and acquire food, this also made genetic sense. But today we fight more with our minds than our muscles, and face challenges that require a strong community building prowess. We therefore need to consign old female and male roles to the fading pages of history.

* * *

HOPE & SLOW PROGRESS

I am writing this chapter during the 2012 Olympics. These are the first games in which all participating teams have female competitors, and have subsequently been heralded as a significant first for female equality. Just a month before the Olympics began, Maria das Graças Foster also became the CEO of Petrobras, and hence the first women to run one of the world's top five oil companies. Look back a year earlier to June 2011, and Christine Lagarde was just taking up her role as the first female head of the International Monetary Fund.

These three examples are all indicators of progress and have to be welcomed as good news. Yet the fact that these firsts have happened so recently is equally a sign that very significant progress still needs to be made. There is no doubt that the struggle to get more women into notable and powerful positions continues to accrue fresh victories. But the battle for female equality on so many fronts is still very far from won.

For example, on average a woman doing the same job as a man still earns less than her male counterpart. At least in financial terms, global civilization therefore continues to value women less than men. As recently as September 2011, a woman in Saudi Arabia was even sentenced to ten lashes for driving a vehicle.[150] When any society is prepared to so brutally punish a woman for such a 'crime', it is perhaps difficult to imagine that they will anytime soon work to achieve an even gender balance across all levels of authority.

We should therefore not forget that less than a century ago women did not have the vote, with history subsequently teaching us that seemingly impossible reforms are possible, and all societies capable of positive and radical change.

At the start of this chapter I noted that many futurists believe the future to be female. This is also a sentiment with which I heartily agree. Given the evidence presented in this chapter, I also hope that the benefits of having more women in authority are something that many men and many companies will at least start to seriously contemplate.

Still today, most of those who argue that more females should hold top jobs do so on the grounds of sexual equality and the right of all women to self determination. From a human rights perspective this is a very solid argument. Yet of even more importance is the broader need for human civilization to introduce a female perspective into its decision making structures in order to craft the best possible future for us all. We therefore all need to work to change the gender balance of our society if we want tomorrow to turn out the way that most sane people would desire.

7

THE DEATH OF ECONOMICS

One Sunday afternoon last May I spoke at a Greenbelt Festivals event in central London. This consisted of ten short talks in which a number of campaigners, clergy, writers – and one futurist – offered their take on how paradise has been lost, and how it just might be recovered.

The event was video recorded at All Hallows on the Wall church. This is only a stone's throw from the shimmering glass of London's iconic Gherkin building, and the cold, old stone of the Bank of England. The location was therefore ironic given that not one speaker had anything complimentary to say about bankers or our current economic and financial system. Rather, in our very different ways, all of us ended up providing a critique of capitalism, with paradise never once presented as having any monetary or economic foundation.

The last talk was given by writer, broadcaster, priest and poet Martin Wroe. Just one of the things that made his presentation so compelling was that he used a lot of props. As Martin recounted the tale of an old woman who sat knitting while watching television, he held up her needles and wool. He then showed us several of the garments she had made for her future grandchildren. Martin also reminded us that, since the 15th century, generations of women have sat patiently knitting, thinking and almost meditating to the clickety-click rhythm of their needles.

After a few minutes, Martin presented a particularly intricate baby's jumper and pointed out that, if the old lady who made it had been paid the minimum wage, it would 'have to go on sale for £180'. This was unfortunate given that a similar, more durable and stain-resistant garment could be purchased from Mothercare for under £10. As Martin reflected, the woman was not viable. Her work was simply unsustainable. She was 'not a going concern and never would be'.[151]

Martin gently proceeded to point out that the old woman was not actually producing a cardigan. Rather, she was making a gift. She loved the process of creation, and the thought that someone she cared for would soon be wearing something she had made. Economics had not even entered her head when she took the decision to knit. And as Martin's audience silently nodded in mutual agreement, nobody would ever have expected it to.

PROVOKING DEBATE

As you have probably noticed, I have called this chapter 'The Death of Economics'. This title is I know controversial, and not least among some of my economist colleagues in the University of Nottingham. However, my intention in using the 'Death of Economics' moniker is absolutely *to be controversial* and to provoke potentially uncomfortable debate.

As Martin Wroe's Greenbelt presentation made clear, economic logic does not lie at the heart of many of the things we truly value. Economics and monetary exchange ought really to be no more than just one, formal mechanism for facilitating the allocation of physical resources and human time. And yet somehow, in the Modern Age, we appear to have forgotten that.

In calling for the 'death of economics', I am proposing that we ought to stop relying so heavily on traditional economic logic as the primary decision making mechanism of human civilization. Today, more people believe in the power of economics than in any one church, with economists worshipped in the media and by most politicians as all-knowing gods. We also now collectively place the welfare of the economy above the failing health of the planetary ecosystem that keeps our species alive. Community and equality are additionally frequently trampled by out-of-control market forces.

The above I believe to be wrong. And it is for this reason that I am writing this final chapter under the 'Death of Economics' banner. As I noted in chapter 5, some pioneering crowdsourcing communities are already championing non-profit and even non-financial mechanisms for delivering at least some of the goods, services and support that people need. Potential alternatives to the way we currently run the world are therefore starting to be figured out, and I will indeed explore a few more of them later in this chapter.

Before I progress my argument, I need to stress that I am not proposing the scrapping of all economic mechanisms. People do, after all, rely on monetary exchange to live. Companies also have to understand and manage their incomes and expenditures or they will not remain in business very long. Even governments eventually have to pay their monetary way (even if many across Europe currently seem to have forgotten this inconvenient fact).

As somebody who spent seven years studying economics at school and university – and who even spent a couple of years tutoring the subject at degree level – I am also not suggesting that people should not learn about economic principles. Economics is a solid discipline as far as it goes, and as such a potentially useful social science to study providing that its relevance to the modern world is kept in perspective. On a basic, business level, price does have to meet or exceed cost or things will rapidly go wrong. Although, as Martin Wroe reminds us, even this equation only holds true in those totally commercial spheres in which we do not spend the majority of our lives.

The more that we live more locally, use less energy, repair broken items, dematerialize, crowdsource, and place more women in authority, the more activities are also likely to cross from the commercial to the non-commercial side of the line. Economics therefore needs to be relegated back to being just one tool in our decision making arsenal, rather than continuing to serve as the driving force of human civilization.

IMAGINING AN ALTERNATIVE

For anybody brought up in the West – myself very much included – it is extremely difficult to even imagine any system of decision making and resource allocation that does not place economic principles at its heart. Rising to this challenge, within the worlds of *Star Trek: The Next Generation*, Gene Roddenberry attempted to show us what it may be like by conjuring up a science fiction future in which money did not exist. To cite Captain Picard:

> The economics of the future are somewhat different. You see, money doesn't exist in the 24th century. . . . The acquisition of wealth is no longer the driving force in our lives. We work to better ourselves, and the rest of humanity.[152]

Unfortunately, beyond these fine words, just quite how resources came to be allocated was hardly made clear, with the operation of the *Star Trek* post-economic paradise never really explained. In fact, by the time that sister show *Star Trek: Deep Space Nine* was created, a currency called 'gold pressed latinum' had to be introduced to allow for storylines based around corruption and trade.

The above teaches us that even science fiction writers find it hard to remain detached from the structural mechanisms associated with traditional economic principles. Today, most of us are brainwashed from an early age into believing that Economics is King, and it is very difficult to step aside from that programming.

One of the reasons that the status quo is so hard to even conceptually escape is that our civilization has for centuries relied on an established foundation of educational knowledge. Much of this knowledge – including information and expertise relating to medicine, building construction, transportation, communications and power generation – is essential for the continued functioning of modern society. Each generation stands on the shoulders of the one that gave birth to it, and would simply not have time to reinvent the wheel and everything else if we stopped formally teaching people physics, chemistry, biology, engineering and so many other critical things. The 'knowledge economy' is indeed not a recent invention as many claim, but something that has been thriving since at least the Industrial Revolution.

There is, however, always a problem. And here the spanner in the works is that we continue to build our society not just on the foundation of past science, but on the bedrock of far more dubious past *social science* as well. As a result, upcoming generations continue to rote-learn unquestioned techniques for running countries, economies and companies that are not necessarily correct. Some of what is relentlessly taught may have been applicable in days gone by. But to be honest, many of the economic principles that are still preached as universal truths were probably never correct.

For example, it never, ever made sense to build systems of global trade that are entirely dependent on a finite and constantly diminishing supply of petroleum. Nor was ignoring the implications of pollution ever a remotely sensible or 'sustainable' proposition. It is just that, before the human race got so big and started to hit the physical limits of our first planet, the flaws in our collective, economic logic never became apparent.

Not that many centuries ago, most 'educated' people were taught that the world was flat. But they were wrong, and dangerously so if they ended up giving you global sailing directions. The same is also true when it comes to the indoctrinated belief in traditional economic mechanisms that is still drilled into so many potentially smart people today.

Great universities keep on churning out fresh-faced future politicians and business leaders with good economics and related degrees. But this in no way implies that the people they have 'educated' have relevant knowledge and know what they are doing, anymore than people who thought the world was flat ought to have been trusted in days gone by. We live in a world that has to unquestionably believe in what our education systems teach, because without modern education we could simply not survive. It is therefore unfortunate that we also fall foul of the trust we place in formal education systems if and when they end up perpetually teaching large numbers of people the wrong things.

History informs us that times are always hard when long-held beliefs need to be completely cast aside. Many people seriously got their proverbial knickers in a twist when Nicolaus Copernicus presented his theory that the Earth revolved around the Sun and not the other way around. But he was right, and in time those who believed him ceased to be burnt at the stake and the majority worldview changed. In a similar fashion, Victorian England took a great deal of convincing that human beings had descended from apes (and not from Adam and Eve) as some vile creature named Charles Darwin ridiculously claimed.

I mention all of the above to highlight the intense conceptual challenge that is involved when something as sacred as traditional economic logic is even questioned. I regularly find myself thinking 'but how else could things *really* work?', and I have been contemplating post-economic civilization for some time. Thinking outside of the box of economic 'rationality' is extremely difficult. Yet this is exactly what we all somehow increasingly need to do.

SLAYING THE SACRED COWS

There are in essence five key reasons why traditional economic decision making will increasingly fail us all. In short, the problems are that constant growth is mandated, externalities are ignored, physical globalization is pursued, human values are trampled, and environmental challenges cannot be resolved. I will now explore each of these interrelated issues in turn.

THE FOLLY OF CONSTANT GROWTH

As I have stressed several times in this book, the number one problem with conventional economics is its unquestioned requirement for constant economic growth. To state that economic growth is the obsession of almost all governments and financial markets is hardly to overstate the point. As top economists and other commentators bleat in the media almost daily, economic growth creates jobs and prevents stagnation. A constantly growing economy also results in some level of inflation. This then helps governments to pay off their debts, as by the time their long-term bonds mature they are worth far less in real terms.

The above all sounds marvellous. It also explains why most people and politicians still buy-in to the belief that constant economic growth is essential and ought to be pursued at all costs. It is therefore somewhat sad that the whole idea is ludicrous, dangerous, and if left unchecked will soon have devastating implications for all life on this planet.

In biology there is a special and often feared word for anything that grows relentlessly. And that word is cancer. We all know that something is wrong if an adult creature starts to grow uncontrollably, and that a lifecycle of birth, growth and stable maturity is the most natural state of affairs. It is therefore quite bizarre that we have somehow convinced ourselves that our economies are immune from this natural cycle and can expand indefinitely.

As renowned biologist David Suzuki states in his book *The Legacy*, raising the human-created entity called the economy above the survival of the biosphere is suicidal. As he argues, 'the services performed by nature should be our highest concern for our own self-interest because they enable animals like us to survive and flourish, but they are ignored by conventional economics'.[153]

To develop David Suzuki's point, it is worth remembering the common saying that 'the most important thing anybody can have is their health'. This is also true not just for an individual, but for the whole of humanity. After all, unless we look after the welfare of the biosphere we are all in deep trouble regardless of how big or small the financial economy happens to be. It therefore makes extreme sense for us to reject our current, delusional 'requirement' for endless economic growth, and to find ways to consume less, value more, and return the living system of our first planet to full health. In fact, if we do not do this, we are condemning the generations of tomorrow to an early grave.

But what, some people may cry, about the popular new mantra of 'sustainable economic growth'? Surely that is the road to our salvation?

Well for a start, as I explained in chapter 2, it is a thermo-dynamic certainty that nothing can ever be entirely sustainable. So at best the magical, modern alternative to 'constant economic growth' that many politicians talk about should be labelled 'constant *more sustainable* economic growth'. This is also really no different to constant economic growth, if at a slightly more leisurely pace. We really cannot sensibly seek to protect the biosphere and to conserve resources while pursuing any form of economic expansion. To fix the world we have no choice but to pursue a stable or shrinking traditional economy.

A stable economy? Or even a shrinking one? Am I kidding?! Well no I am not. Moreover, we really need to stop fearing a stable or shrinking economy as a terrible thing. In fact, if we started to live more locally, to pursue low energy lifestyles, to dematerialize, to maintain rather than discard broken items, and to crowdsource more open source products, we could probably maintain our standard of living while spending less money in an economy of a significantly smaller size. This does not mean that we could continue to buy as much stuff as we do today, to have so much choice, or to travel so widely. But we could continue to eat, be sheltered, work, play and globally communicate as materially well as we currently do, if in a somewhat different manner.

In developing nations with a low standard of living, the pursuit of economic growth may still be championed as a moral cause. In most nations, however, it is no longer something that can remotely be justified. All developed economies now have in aggregate enough wealth, working hours, wages and salaries to provide all of their citizens with a decent standard of living. Granted, some redistribution of these assets is required if the chasm between rich and poor is to be closed. But we must not be fooled into believing that the pursuit of constant economic growth will bring about such a redistribution. In fact, as many nations have industrialized, the gap between their richest and poorest citizens has widened rather than decreased. By its very nature, economic growth is simply not a driver of equality and ethical practice. Nor is it sustainable, or something that the citizens of most nations actually require.

EXTERNALITIES IGNORED

Closely linked to the fundamental folly of a belief in constant economic growth is the way in which conventional economics assumes away 'externalities'. This means that conventional economics focuses only on things to which it chooses to give a short-term monetary value. The broader consequences of most economic activities are then simply ignored.

For example, pollution, resource depletion, climate change, and the welfare of future generations, are not given a price. Rather, they are gleefully ignored in the name of short-term greed and profit. As David Suzuki argues, it is only by paying no attention to the ecological costs of our actions that it has become possible for us to believe in the impossible fantasy of constant economic growth.[154] Or as Graeme Maxton laments in his book *The End of Progress*, every year humanity destroys more than it builds, with the global economy growing by about $1.5 trillion annually, but environmental damage to the planet running at an estimated $4.5 trillion. Traditional economic practices are therefore causing us to 'evolve backwards' as we consistently lay waste to more than we create.[155]

It is also not just environmental externalities that get casually assumed away. The financial troubles that much of the world continues to bear are equally the result of those with economic hearts and minds choosing to ignore the wider implications of their actions. The financial markets took great pleasure in fabricating new commodities like credit default swaps and amalgamated sub-prime debt, and then proceeded to recklessly trade in them without a thought to the consequences of failure. This non-priced consequence then nearly bankrupted us all.

The whole discipline of economics just assumes away anything problematic – and then acts all surprised and coy when it gets caught out. For years I attended academic seminars at which leading economists from other universities came to showcase their latest work to colleagues at Nottingham. On many occasions I would question the naïve assumptions that they made about the world, and which they usually brushed over in the first few minutes of their talk. My learned colleagues would then frown, the presenter would move on, and a 'proper' debate would take place regarding the intricate mathematics included right at the end of the presentation.

Believe me, this really is how top-level economics is practised, and how many economists as supposedly intelligent people behave. They play the game of ignoring inconvenient but very real truths – like pollution, 'irrational' human emotion and finite resources – just so that their fantasy worldview can survive and 'develop' without a scratch. (I have of course long since given up attending such seminars).

Economics is simply incapable of doing anything about the consequence behind the price. To cite another example, today in the United States there are so many 'dead zones' in rivers and coastal waters that 80 per cent of the country's seafood has to be imported. The reason? An overuse of oil-based pesticides is creating toxic agricultural runoff. This is, however, no problem for economists, as farmers have increased their yields, a profit is being made, and somebody overseas can also earn a profit by selling fish to the United States. Many others can in turn make a profit by transporting the globally imported fish, and by providing petroleum to fuel the boats and lorries that carry it. In economic terms, everything is just great, with everybody winning. Well, except for the absent and poisoned American fish and the planet, and they do not have a bank account.

You may think that I am getting cynical here, and perhaps I am. Even so, a system of trading and living that freely pollutes, exploits and ignores tomorrow is exactly what we have created for ourselves due to our overwhelming reliance on conventional economic logic.

To fix the world, we have to start collectively remembering that just because we *can* economically afford to do something does not mean that we actually *should*. We also need to begin acting in the knowledge that just because something is cheaper, it is not necessarily better or more desirable if that reduced monetary price is imposing high and uncalculated costs on the planet and our children's children. As I keep stressing, it really is time for us to start making non-economic decisions that will cause us to consume things less and value things more.

FAILING GLOBALIZATION

Another very major issue with current economic logic is its obsession with a mass global trade in physical things. I said a lot about this madness in chapter 1, so will just provide a brief reminder of the issue here. In short, globalization only works because it relies on the consumption of rapidly depleting fossil fuels to move gargantuan quantities of stuff around the planet.

As Graeme Maxton argues, many modern economic notions relating to free trade, competition and regulation really need to be reconsidered.[156] Since Adam Smith wrote *The Wealth of Nations* back in 1776, economists have campaigned for 'free markets' with virtually unrestricted trade and very light regulation. In the past few decades, such damn foolishness has also been taken far further than even Adam Smith could ever have imagined or probably even desired.

For Smith, free trade between countries was something to be championed to improve the well-being of a country's citizens. It is therefore unfortunate that the mania of globalization today often achieves exactly the opposite result. For a start, people in poor nations get exploited to produce cheap goods for those in rich countries, with economic forces also causing scarce food and water to be transported away from those who most need it. As mass globalization has taken hold, the planet's resources have also been squandered, while our climate has gradually warmed in line with skyrocketing fossil fuel usage.

In environmental and many other terms, it does not make sense for any nation – or indeed any large region – to import food and other basic goods if they could be produced locally. This is not to suggest that all nations ought to return to the highly protectionist trading practices of decades gone by. But it absolutely would make sense to permit countries to at least partially protect their farmers, as well as their manufacturers of basic or strategic goods including machine tools, clothing, home appliances, healthcare supplies and vehicles.

By reducing the global trade in basic items – if continuing to globalize their design and a trade in some of their high-value components – human civilization could dramatically reduce fossil fuel usage. In the process we could also finally make progress in the battle against global warming. For most of human history, globally imported goods were usually non-essential luxuries. We now need to return to that state of affairs before it is too late.

TRAMPLING HUMAN VALUES

The widespread practice of traditional economics was one of the greatest blessings but also the greatest blights of the 20th century. As capitalism won the battle against communism, both governments and business became narrow-minded as economic logic came to dominate so much of world thought. The very positive result was that prosperity ensued. But the very negative implication was that economics-first decision making trod all-too-heavily over so many of those human values that allowed us to survive long before coin, note and e-banking website.

Nowhere has the curse of blind economic logic been felt so disastrously as across the eurozone. Indeed, the fact that 14 independent countries – whose citizens never voted for political union – are now commonly referred to as a basket case collective says it all.

After the Second World War, a load of concerned political men in suits got together to dream up a means of preventing another war. The 'common market' they ended up inventing may have been created with the best of intentions. But this beast of cancerous economic logic has in recent years brought Continental Europe to its knees all over again. It may have taken several decades to get most member states of the European Economic Community (as it used to be called) to junk their national sovereignty by slaving themselves to a single currency. But the plan worked, and the whole world continues to be sucked toward the abyss by the colossal folly of the euro.

At best, those who built the eurozone did so in the naïve belief that cementing together 14 totally different economies would lead to harmonious prosperity. They also hoped that, by straight-jacketing the peoples of Continental Europe to a single economic path, broader political and cultural union could be sneakily implemented against most citizens' wishes.

The mess than has resulted is truly ghastly, and not just for the poor souls in Greece, Spain, Ireland and Portugal whose local economics have been trashed in the name of Europe-wide economic good.

If people in the future ever need a reminder of how putting economics first will eventually result in failure, they will only need to look back to the calamity of the eurozone. Almost certainly, people will be pointing wisely back to its disaster for centuries. Just as constant economic growth is in the long run completely unachievable, so any long-term 'economics first and everything else second' solution simply does not work.

Back in December 1998, I remember attending a meal at the end of a two-day workshop that I had been facilitating for a number of UK banks and other financial services organizations. At this time, the euro was about to be launched, and several top bankers at the table were bemoaning bitterly how stupid the United Kingdom was for not taking part.

As several of them told me, as a country we had made the 'wrong economic decision'. I countered that maybe such an important decision ought not to be made entirely on an economic basis, and received some very strange looks. When I then explained that the United Kingdom had sensibly placed cultural identity and self-determination first, almost all of the bankers present were just bemused. We did not even get into the argument that, without the tight political and fiscal integration that nobody across Europe would agree to, the whole euro project was doomed to fail somewhere down the line.

As individuals all know, and as governments and organizations really ought to be aware, human beings affiliate to and worry about a great many things, and the majority of these are not financial. I am not here suggesting that money is not important and does not matter to most people, and especially to those in financial hardship. Yet increasingly, those who can afford the basic essentials of living are as concerned about their family and friends, their health, the environment, ethical practices, their sense of identity, and their religion, as they are about always getting the best price or behaving with pure economic rationality.

The fact that politicians across Europe dare not hold referendums to progress their economically-founded super-state provides just one example of how ordinary people are known to be 'rebelling' against economics-first thinking. The Irish prime minister – who in 2008 was constitutionally forced to hold a referendum on the EU Lisbon Treaty – may have publicly apologized to the EU when his electorate made the 'wrong economic decision'. But I would guess that, fairly soon, politicians will not be able to go on blaming their citizens for not believing in the Religion of Economics.

In 1973, a guy called Fritz Schumacher wrote an enlightened book called *Small Is Beautiful: Economics as if People Mattered*. This questioned any requirement for constant economic growth, and suggested that small scale technologies are better than bigger, more environmentally-destructive machines. The book also proposed that 'saturating' ourselves in material wealth is self-defeating, with a 'serious shift' needed in the modern perception of 'progress'.[157]

Originally in this chapter I had intended to review Schumacher's work in some depth. But then it struck me that the title of his book really says it all. For decades we have run the world based on a system of economic logic that has ignored the deeper human and cultural implications of its practice. The phrase 'economics as if people mattered' is to most of us an oxymoron. And this accounts for a great many of the challenges that we all now have to deal with.

Environmental Failings

When it comes to helping us deal with fundamental environmental problems, conventional economic mechanisms simply do not work. Climate change and broader resource depletion are beyond traditional economic comprehension. Indeed, the Stern Review on climate change produced for the UK government freely admitted that 'climate change is the greatest and widest-ranging market failure ever seen'.[158] The way that it then proceeded to make proposals based on economic logic was at best bizarre.

'But no!' some flat-Earth, economics-first advocates cry, 'the market can fix everything if we implement new subsidies and mechanisms such as carbon trading'. Well, I am sorry, but again this is balderdash.

Many economists argue that subsidies are needed to encourage individuals and companies to switch to green technologies. Having bought this idea, some countries now offer generous subsidies to promote the uptake of solar panels and wind turbines. In some respects this is a good thing. But the end result is basically to give away taxpayers' money to allow a small number of people to buy low-efficiency means of power generation.

For example, many of the PV solar panels now appearing on domestic rooftops have very low net energy yields. Even so, in the United Kingdom people have been racing to fit them. Why? Because the guaranteed government subsidies on the electricity they can return to the national grid have given rooftop PV panels a better return-on-investment than money left in the bank. PV subsidies have therefore been doing nothing to change attitudes to energy usage. Nor are people being encouraged to switch to alternative energy sources because it is the right thing to do.

It will always be impossible to subsidize things for everybody. Public money therefore ought to be directed into green technology research and development, rather than economic fantasies that permit a minority of canny, cash-rich souls to turn a profit.

As guru climate scientist James Lovelock argues, green technology simply does not need a subsidy. Instead, the thing we need to address is our system of resource allocation that signals some things as not worth doing because they are not 'economic'.[159] The more subsidies we 'need', the more we are really acknowledging the failure of our economic system. We should therefore stop trying to make things artificially economically viable, and instead focus on making at least some decisions on a non-economic basis.

Carbon trading is an even more flawed if common economic 'solution' to the global challenge of climate change. The system 'works' by allocating greenhouse gas emission quotas to industrial polluters. A market is then opened up in which those who have less carbon emissions than their quota or cap can sell their 'unused' carbon credits to other polluters. In effect, carbon trading allows many of those who emit greenhouse gases to carry on regardless by using market mechanisms to economically shift their carbon footprint somewhere else.

Since 37 industrialized nations signed up to the Kyoto Protocol in 1997, carbon trading has been at the centre of global climate policy. The trade in carbon credits is also developing into one of the world's largest commodities markets. And yet, as Carbon Trade Watch researchers Tamra Gilbertson and Oscar Reyes explain, the whole multibillion dollar scheme has failed to change how energy is acquired and used, while short-circuiting demands for fundamental reforms, and 'rewarding polluters for continued pollution'.[160]

The above is also not surprising. After all, the whole premise of carbon trading is to allow polluters to pay someone else to clean up their mess so that they do not have to. It should also be quite obvious that setting up a market in the new commodity of carbon credits was 'bound to be an invitation to traders to focus their ingenuity on profit-seeking even if the results undermine climatic stability'.[161] We need to get everybody to reduce their emissions, rather than allowing some companies and even countries to justify their high emissions by 'offsetting' them against better practice elsewhere.

The largest carbon trading scheme in the world is the European Union Emissions Trading Scheme (EU ETS). This covers 11,500 power stations, factories and refineries across all 27 EU member states, plus Norway, Iceland and Lichtenstein. As with all such schemes, beyond its flawed premise of allowing some polluters to dodge their responsibility in exchange for money, other problems have become apparent.

For example, the initial allocation of 'emission allowances' proved extremely problematic. Not least this was because initial free allowances were based on historical emissions. While this may at first have seemed fair, in practice it just resulted in the most inefficient and polluting factories being given the largest emissions quotas.[162] Those who had invested in greener plants were therefore penalized, with an economic 'solution' once again failing to deliver.

Just like recycling, carbon trading is a nice little fantasy that allows those unprepared to change their ways to feel a bit better about destroying the lives of people in the future. Yet it fails completely to address the fact that economic mechanisms will never lead companies away from short-term, me-first decision making. Climate change and resource depletion ought not to be a profit opportunity. And until this is accepted, progress in dealing with these monumental challenges is likely to remain impeded.

THE ROAD AHEAD

As the previous sections have hopefully shown, we cannot continue to run the world solely using for-profit market mechanisms. Economics must therefore be at least partially cast aside. The question is, how may this be achieved and by whom?

At the highest level, it is up to governments to start putting economic mechanisms second. For example, to briefly return to the issue of reducing energy usage and curtailing green-house gas emissions, governments could simply decide to fine those companies that exceed ever-decreasing carbon caps. This would force every firm to behave responsibly, with no opportunities for any business to avoid dealing with their own emissions. Such an approach would also not allow profits to be generated from new forms of 'green trading'.

While brave politicians may in time implement these kinds of measures, we absolutely cannot rely on govern-ments to fix the world. At least in a democracy, any funda-mental revolution has to start at a grass roots level. The gradual demise of economics therefore has to depend on the collective efforts of us all.

To some extent, we can make a start by pursuing the six other ways to fix the world covered in the rest of this book. In time, as individuals and companies pursue more local living, low energy lifestyles and the other things I have mentioned, so the values of our society will change, and politicians will slowly start to pick up on this.

We have to remember that politicians only get elected on the promise of popular (or least worst) policies. Until there is a groundswell of opinion away from the modern mantra of economics-first decision making, we hence cannot realis-tically expect politics to radically change. This said, with the rise of the anti-capitalist Occupy Movement, and a growing awareness of the many future challenges we now face, there is at least some hope that mainstream politicians may start to get elected on a post-economics mandate before the end of the decade.

FUTURE SOLUTIONS?

Beyond broad hopes and generalities, a few dreamers, thinkers and shapers are now trying to figure out very specific ways to challenge the economic status quo. The following sections will therefore detail a few of their ideas. In part I am presenting these initiatives to highlight their existence and individual progress. But far more significantly, I am including them here to illustrate how alternatives to traditional economic mechanisms are already being developed and championed. It will probably take some time before any of the following are refined enough for widespread implementation. Even so, each and every pioneer deserves our support and thanks for at least proactively trying to be part of the solution.

LOCAL MONEY

Conventional economics promotes free trade, and ideally on an unconstrained global basis. As, however, I have already argued, reducing opportunities for free trade may in some circumstances have very positive consequences. Taking this idea to its extreme, some pioneering communities are now experimenting with local money that can only be spent in their own, small geographic region.

The potential problem with national currencies is that they transfer wealth from poor to rich regions. They also inevitably fuel globalization. In contrast, local currencies circulate wealth within their own town or small geographic area. They may therefore promote more local, more resilient and more sustainable modes of living.

When businesses accept payment in a local currency, they are inevitably encouraged to trade with local rather than national or global suppliers. In fact, it can be argued that true localization is impossible without a local currency to back it up.

Local money advocate Peter North argues that while a national unit of exchange is very useful, it needs a complementary local currency running alongside it. As he explains, national currencies often fail, as they:

> . . . often feel like something done to communities. The large corporate chains that now dominate the nation's high streets are like mining operations, extracting the potential wealth of communities and siphoning it away to shareholders and executive bonuses. It is a vicious cycle: people buy from chain stores, less money goes to local businesses, less money circulates locally, [and] local businesses struggle. . . . A local currency is an intervention that can, it is hoped, start to reverse that trend, building trade for local businesses, creating a mindfulness that means people start to choose local shops over chains, and encouraging them to get out and discover the independent traders in their community.[163]

Some of the Transition Initiatives mentioned in chapter 2 have been the first to introduce local monetary systems. For example, in September 2009, Transition Town Brixton in the United Kingdom launched the Brixton pound as 'money that sticks to Brixton'.[164] At launch this was accepted by 70 local traders. The currency was also backed by the local council, who were prepared to accept rent and Council Tax payments in Brixton pounds.

Across the United Kingdom, local currencies have also been launched in Totnes, Lewes, Stroud, and most recently Bristol. As the website for the latter explains:

As more and more shoppers and businesses spend the Bristol Pound, it [keeps] more of people's hard earned wages in our communities to be spent again. People in Bristol who love the range of independent traders [put] their money where it matters and reduce the need for lorries constantly moving goods up and down the country. The scheme is also a powerful way to promote local businesses trading with each other.[165]

Worldwide, several hundred local money and local exchange trading systems (LETS) now exist. All have the community goals of promoting localization and keeping wealth within their local region. They also strongly signal a growing realization that economic systems ought to serve their users, and not the other way around.

ACHIEVING STEADY STATE

A few organizations do now recognize that constant economic growth is impossible on a planet with finite resources. One of these is the Center for the Advancement of the Steady State Economy (CASSE), which has published an impressive document called *Enough Is Enough*. This it describes as 'the single most complete collection of policy initiatives, tools, and reforms' that would result in a zero-growth economy focused not on making more, but simply enough.[166]

Enough Is Enough suggests that global and local caps should be set on the use of specific resources based on the best information available about ecological limits. It also suggests that governments ought to take non-coercive measures to stabilize their populations, and that efforts should be make to democratize workplaces and other institutions where inequalities originate. To this end, employee ownership and cooperatives are encouraged, along with 'progressive taxation and generous social programmes' to reduce inequality and eliminate poverty.

Enough Is Enough also proposes that 'private banks should be prohibited from creating money out of thin air', with public authorities (such as central banks) solely able to 'decide the amount of money necessary to facilitate exchange in the economy'. In tandem, there are proposals for progress to be measured not in GDP, but via new indicators that signal the achievement of sustainable goals and 'equitable human well being'. CASSE also advocates the pursuit of full employment by shortening the working week; that companies ought to pursue 'right-sized' rather than maximum profits; and that attempts need to be made to replace mass consumer culture with a new 'mass behaviour of enoughness'.[167]

There can be no doubt that *Enough Is Enough* is a highly comprehensive policy statement that – if enacted – could potentially go a long way to fix many of the world's problems. My only real criticism is that it appears to place a great deal of trust in the ability of governments to deliver many of the measures it proposes. This I am sceptical about simply because centralist command-and-control economies have never worked in the past. This said, *Enough Is Enough* is a bold document and well worth a read.

A RESOURCE-BASED ECONOMY

Another far larger organization that is working on solutions for a radically new kind of world is the Zeitgeist Movement. This is a 'global sustainability advocacy group' that has over 1,000 Regional Chapters working across 70 countries, and which urges change in the 'dominant intellectual, moral and cultural climate of our time'.[168] As the Movement's website explains:

> . . . each Chapter works to not only spread awareness about the roots of our social problems today but also to express the logical, scientific solutions and methods we have at our

disposal to update and correct the current social system and create a truly responsible, sustainable, peaceful, global society. Working through global and regional educational projects and community programs, the intermediate goal is to obtain a worldwide movement, essentially unifying the people, regardless of country, religion or political party, with a common value identification that we all invariably share, pertaining to our survival and sustainability.[169]

Key to the Zeitgeist Movement's thinking is the development of a 'resource-based economic model'. This is the idea of taking a 'direct technical approach to social management as opposed to a Monetary or even Political one'. This will involve 'updating the workings of society to the most advanced and proven methods Science has to offer', so leaving behind the damaging consequences of our 'current system of monetary exchange, profits [and] corporations'.[170]

In contrast to the polices proposed by the Centre for the Advancement of the Steady State Economy, the Zeitgeist Movement very much believes – as I do – that any revolution in pursuit of a post-economics world needs to first gather momentum at a grass roots level. Once enough awareness and debate has been raised, transformative social and cultural ideas will then gradually take hold across governments, businesses and those other established power structures that make and implement humanity's big decisions. Once again, this implies that we all have a responsibility to become more informed and, having become so, to communicate and engage in the kinds of planetary debate that the Internet now makes possible. Or as I used to say at the end of my YouTube videos, 'the future rests in all of our hands'.

* * *

THE MASTERS OF DELUSION

Most people in developed nations have to bear at least some responsibility for the perpetuation and failings of our economics-focused civilization. This said, it also has to be true that those who preach and practise traditional economics are a little bit more responsible than others. Similarly, those who keep appointing economists to positions of authority must inevitably bear a fair proportion of the blame for our current and potential-future woes. Economic theory does not, after all, arrive and get implemented all by itself. I would therefore respectfully suggest that most individuals who label themselves as mainstream 'economists' – as well as those who employ them – ought to start questioning their professional belief system and the resultant policies they advocate.

Financial institutions, governments and others will probably always need at least *some* economists to help them interpret what is happening monetarily in the world. But we really should not forget that the economy needs economists about as much as hurricanes need weather forecasters. Neither economists or weather forecasters will ever be in actual or apparent control, and nor should they be.

During more than two decades in academia, I have known and worked with many economists. All have been very decent people and hardly the sort of individuals that anybody would fear. Unfortunately, the same could probably also be said of those who once believed in a flat planet.

Across history, millions of good people have come to believe in dubious practices that have brought much suffering. Before anybody spotted the problem, they could also not reasonably be held to account for their misguided beliefs and associated actions. For example, those in the last century who fitted asbestos building materials did not proceed with bad intent. Nevertheless, as evidence mounts against any lost cause, so at the very least the common sense of those who continue to cling to its outdated model of reality has to be seriously questioned.

Forgive me for suggesting that economists are stupid. But really, how much confidence can we sensibly place in any narrow-minded cult which believes the best way out of a debt crisis is to borrow more money? Or that, as a result of globalization, it is sensible for food to travel thousands of miles to our plate? Or that finite natural resources can support *constant* economic growth?

Right now, we would have more success with the animals of Narnia in charge. Just how we have let the Masters of Delusion stay in control for so long is mystifying. Except that it is not – as the economists are, if nothing else, the Masters of Delusion.

Like so many true believers, economists have become addicted to their own cause. This means that, even when they are proved wrong, they simply twist their worldview to try and explain why things are not turning out as they economically should.

Admittedly we all have a confirmation bias. We may all also live more easily if we never challenge what we believe (or have been told to believe). But none of this makes things right. It is therefore now time to give the economists notice that they are in the sunset of their reign. Granted, exactly how a post-economics world will function is still very far from clear. But we can be absolutely certain that economics-first thinking is just making things worse and worse. The time has therefore come for us all to jump ship.

EPILOGUE

While I was writing this book, a very intelligent friend asked what it was all about. After we had discussed the contents for some time, he then made two rather perceptive observations. The first was that this book really ought to be called *Seven Ways that in Combination Will Fix the World*, as the seven 'fixes' presented herein are not alternatives. I could also not technically disagree with this feedback, although my friend had to admit that it would have been a less catchy title!

My friend's second observation related to the fact that nothing can ever be sustainable. Noting this, he concluded that – in the long term – my seven ways to fix the world will not actually work. Rather, they will merely extend the period of time before our inevitable decline.

This second observation is probably also true. Indeed, unless humanity somehow manages to start harvesting resources from other planets, my friend's second observation is thermodynamically undeniable. Even so, the fact that we cannot permanently fix the world should not stop us from constantly trying to mend and maintain it.

Everybody is going to die. Yet even in the face of this absolute certainty, doctors do not dismiss the practice of medicine as a futile pursuit. Rather, they continue to treat their patients – not to try and stop them from ever dying, but to prevent their lives from coming to a premature end.

In the same way, what I have presented in this book are seven ways to try and ensure that human civilization fully runs its course. Regardless of the actions we may or may not take, ultimately our civilization will one day come to an end. Even so, we still have a great incentive to try and ensure that the lifespan of advanced humanity is not drastically curtailed by hundreds or thousands of years due to our currently over-indulgent foolishness.

TWO DECADES AND COUNTING

Throughout this book I have stressed that an age of mass scarcity could well be with us as early as 2020, and will almost certainly have arrived by 2030. To back up this assertion, I have drawn on evidence and opinion from the United Nations, the World Bank, several other respected international bodies, and a wide spectrum of scientific studies. Even so, I am aware that many people still do not believe that, within a decade or so, we will have to change our ways.

Back when *The Limits to Growth*[171] was published in 1972, many of its supporters were criticized for suggesting that the Age of Plenty could come to an end anytime soon. In the live-to-excess days of the 1980s and 1990s, they were then mocked further by those who pointed out that the scarcity and wider environmental problems predicted in the 1970s had not occurred.

What the popular critics of *The Limits to Growth* and similar studies somehow missed is that no serious scientist in the 1970s ever suggested that catastrophe would strike in the next decade or even in the one after that. Rather, what they calculated was that we had about half a century of breathing space before things got really tough.

As *The Limits to Growth* received ten year updates, and as other evidence accumulated, many scientists and environmental commentators continued to report that major problems would hit us sometime between 2020 and 2030. The predicted timescales for Peak Everything have therefore never moved, with the '50 years to act' message of the early 1970s dovetailing very consistently with current predictions that we have only one or two decades to environmentally sort ourselves out. The only 'problem' is that environmental and resource depletion issues largely dipped from the mass media radar during the capitalist boom of the 1980s and 1990s.

There really is now very little doubt that, at least in relative terms, an Age of Scarcity is on the fairly near horizon. A harsh or gradual transition to a new way of living is therefore extremely likely to be experienced by most people alive today. We therefore have a great incentive to take steps that may facilitate a soft landing rather than a sudden impact with this medium-term future reality.

Abundance Ahoy?

While many serious commentators believe that an Age of Scarcity will soon be with us, in futurist circles there are very differing views concerning how long it may last. On the one hand, some believe that a long and slow decline is on the cards. This view is based on the assumption that Planet Earth is a closed system with finite natural resources. Under this scenario, and as I posited at the start of this Epilogue, all of the measures outlined in this book ought therefore to be implemented to slow our decline, and to allow advanced human civilization to run its course as comfortably as it can for as long as possible.

On the other hand, some futurists suggest that the second half of this century may turn out to be a new Age of Abundance. This alternative view is based on a belief that, in about half a century's time, we will have accrued so many developments in nanotechnology, synthetic biology, artificial intelligence and other cutting-edge sciences that it will become possible to completely overcome the grand challenges of the next few decades.

As Age of Abundance advocates believe, by around 2050 we may have learnt to use nanotechnology to freely manipulate all matter at its most basic level. This would enable us to turn any collection of atoms into any other, so allowing perfect recycling and preventing future resource scarcity. Sometime in the second half of this century, we may also have mastered the elusive art of producing near-limitless clean power using nuclear fusion.

As I hinted a few pages back, by 2050 we may even have developed a routine space-faring capability that will allow fresh resources to be mined from the Moon or asteroids. This off-world mining may even be undertaken by new species of intelligent robot, or perhaps by servant organic beings conjured into existence using next-generation synthetic biology.

All of the above is fairly common if wild speculation that is nevertheless rooted in an extrapolation of current scientific progress. It therefore actually does have a chance of coming true. However – and it is another of my really big howevers – even if there is a possibility that the pending Age of Scarcity will only last for a few decades, this does not remove the necessity for us to fix the world right now. For a start, we have to survive in the interim. What is more, no hoped-for, high-tech Age of Abundance will be able to emerge from a foundation of nothing. Rather, civilization's industrial second coming only has a chance of succeeding if we manage to maintain both a reasonable stock of natural resources, and a biosphere in a decent state of health.

As both a futurist and an optimist, I would like to think that more responsible living in the next few decades will be rewarded with a new Age of Abundance sometime later this century. OK, so this would be a new dawn that most people alive today would probably not experience. Even so, the possibility that a new mode of industrial civilization may emerge in the future may prove a comforting thought as we enter more difficult times.

In the last century, millions fought in bloody battles and gave their lives to win future freedoms. Implementing the ideas presented in this book will clearly not have to involve anywhere near as significant a sacrifice. Even so, through our actions today we may still contribute to a better future for the inhabitants of tomorrow. In fact, whether or not an Age of Abundance may be on the distant horizon, we can be certain that by acting more responsibly today, we can to some extent improve the lives of those to come.

A NEW NARRATIVE

All civilizations are founded on two pillars. The first is the pillar of their technologies, while the second is the pillar of those stories, myths or narratives that fundamentally determine how people think, dream and behave.

When great technologies and great narratives are combined, the results can be magnificent. For example, when the Ancient Egyptians combined their construction technologies with a religious mantra to immortalize their Pharaohs, they built pyramids that may stand for eternity. Similarly in the 1960s, when the Americans combined their nation's technological might with a belief in their go-getting invincibility, they succeeded in placing a human being on the Moon.

In this book I have outlined how some powerful technologies – including the Internet, 3D printing and synthetic biology – may in the future help us to live in new ways. However, the final thing I want to reflect on is not future technology, but the core narrative of our society and how it needs to change.

Even with crowdsourcing applied, it will take only a relatively few scientists and engineers to create tomorrow's physical and digital machines. In contrast, to shape a new, more sustainable narrative will require the involvement of the majority.

In *The Long Descent*, John Michael Greer beautifully stresses the importance of any civilization's narrative. As he muses:

> We think with myths as inevitably as we see with eyes and eat with mouths. Thus, any attempt to bring about significant social change must start from the mythic level, with an emotionally powerful and symbolically meaningful narrative, or it will go nowhere.[172]

In a sense, the goal of this book has been to help foster a new narrative. Admittedly, each of my proposed seven ways to fix the world involve us practically doing things in new ways. Yet before that, they all first require us to start thinking differently in order to catalyze revised and environmentally healthier actions.

Changing how our civilization thinks and feels, let alone what we collectively believe, is never going to be easy. Not least this is because most of us were never consciously taught the narrative of industrial civilization. Nobody in a school ever stood up to tell us to consume endlessly, to dispose of things needlessly, to favour globalization over localization, and to pursue constant economic growth. Rather, this current narrative slowly soaked into our souls as we were drenched in the dominant structures, mechanisms and media that define the modern world.

To change the narrative of our civilization will require us to start thinking consciously and collectively about what we unconsciously so deeply believe. We will then need to begin questioning those beliefs and propagating new ideologies. At least some of the things we need to start collectively thinking about and debating are the seven ways to fix the world outlined in this book. So when you have finished reading, please talk to people about what you have read. Please also pass this book on to others, or direct them to its free online resources. And above all, please start to proactively get involved in the rising debate. For both me as the author and you as the reader, this book has to help promote change or it will have achieved nothing.

* * *

THE RIGHT SIDE OF THE LINE

While writing this book, I became concerned that it might offend some people. For a while this really bothered me. But then I remembered that, to usefully contribute to any debate about our future, I have to try and stir things up.

If the way we run things right now was working fine, nothing would need to change and we could all continue living just as we do today. But things are not fine, with our 'advanced' civilization running a significant risk of starting to disappear over a proverbial cliff in less than two decades time. If this book has unsettled you in places then that is exactly as it should be. I did not set out to offend (even if you are an economist!). But I did set out to do my part in engendering fairly radical change, and that requires a great deal of conventional thinking to be challenged.

As I said way back in the Prologue, one little book cannot hope to fix the world. But many individuals thinking, dreaming and working together certainly can. We are all now part of the problem or part of the solution. I therefore hope that, if nothing else, this book has prompted you to consider on which side of this divide you intend to spend the remainder of your precious time alive.

NOTES TO ALL CHAPTERS

PROLOGUE

1. Christopher Barnatt *25 Things You Need to Know About the Future* (London: Constable, 2012).

2. *BP Statistical Review of World Energy 2011* (BP, June 2011). Available from: http://bp.com/statisticalreview

3. Steve Sorrell, Jamie Speirs, Roger Bentley, Adam Brandt & Richard Miller *Global Oil Depletion: An Assessment of the Evidence for a Near-term Peak in Global Oil Production* (London: UK Energy Research Centre, 2009).

4. James Lovelock *The Vanishing Face of Gaia* (London: Allen Lane, 2009).

5. Gerald A. Meehl, Julie M. Arblaster, John T. Fasullo, Aixue Hu & Kevin E. Trenberth 'Model-Based Evidence of Deep-Ocean Heat Uptake During Surface-Temperature Hiatus Periods', *Nature Climate Change* Volume 1, pp.360–364. (18 September 2011).

6. United Nations *Water Scarcity* (no date). Available from: http://www.un.org/waterforlifedecade/scarcity.shtml

7. Lester R. Brown, 'How to Feed 8 Billion People', *The Futurist* (January–February 2010).

8. *The Census of Marine Life* (4 October 2010). Available from: http://www.coml.org

9. United Nations Environment Programme *Uncoupling Natural Resource Use and Environmental Impacts from Economic Growth* (Washington, DC: United Nations, May 2011).

10. Donella H. Meadows, Dennis L. Meadows, Jorgen Randers & William W. Behrens III *The Limits to Growth: A Report for the Club of Rome's Project on the Predicament of Mankind* (New York: Universe Books, 1972).

11. Donella H. Meadows, Dennis L. Meadows & Jorgen Randers *Beyond The Limits: Global Collapse or a Sustainable Future* (London: Earthscan Publications, 1992).

12. Donella H. Meadows, Jorgen Randers & Dennis L. Meadows *Limits to Growth: The 30-Year Update* (White River Junction, Vermont: Chelsea

Green Publishing, 2004).

13.   *World Scientists' Warning to Humanity*, (18 November 1992). Available from: http://deoxy.org/sciwarn.htm

14.   Tim O'Reilly *What Is Web 2.0: Design Patterns and Business Models for the Next Generation of Software* (30 September 2005). Available from: http://www.oreillynet.com/lpt/a/6228

15.   Matthew Syed 'What caused the crunch? Men and testosterone', *The Times* (30 September 2008). Available from: http://women.timesonline. co.uk/tol/life_and_style/women/the_way_we_live/article4848188.ece

CHAPTER 1: MORE LOCAL LIVING

16.   Evan Davis *Made in Britain: Episode 1* (London: BBC, 20 June 2011). Further details at: http://www.bbc.co.uk/programmes/b0125v5h

17.   Dickson Despommier *The Vertical Farm: Feeding the World in the 21st Century* (New York, NY: Thomas Dune, 2010).

18.   Good Design *A Former Chicago Meatpacking Plant Becomes a Self-Sustaining Vertical Farm* (23 April 2012). Available from: http://www.good.is/post/a-former-chicago-meatpacking-plant-becomes-a-self-sustaining-vertical-farm/

19.   AlphaFarm *A Big Step Forward* (16 May 2012). Available from: http://alphafarm.org/

20.   our.Windowfarms *Homepage* (no date). Available from: http://our. windowfarms.org/

21.   C.J. Lim & Ed Liu *Smart Cities + Eco-Warriors* (Oxford: Routledge, 2010).

22.   C.J. Lim & Ed Liu, ibid.

23.   Biotech Industry Association *Current Uses of Synthetic Biology* (26 July 2011). Available from: http://www.bio.org/content/current-uses-synthetic-biology

24.   Philip Judkins, David West & John Drew *Networking in Organizations: The Rank Xerox Experiment* (Aldershot: Gower, 1985).

CHAPTER 2: LOW ENERGY LIFESTYLES

25.   *BP Statistical Review of World Energy 2011* (BP, June 2011). Available from: http://bp.com/statisticalreview

26.   *BP Statistical Review of World Energy 2012* (BP, June 2012). Available from: http://bp.com/statisticalreview

27.   US Department of Energy SunShot Initiative (29 June 2012). Available from: http://www1.eere.energy.gov/solar/sunshot/index.html

28.   Bill Sweet 'A Green Energy Scorecard', IEEE Spectrum (18 March 2012). Available from: http://spectrum.ieee.org/energywise/energy/renewables/a-green-energy-scorecard

29. James Lovelock *The Vanishing Face of Gaia* (London: Penguin, 2009).

30. Ideas21 *Energy Return on Energy Invested* (18 June 2012). Available from: http://www.ideas21.co.za/tag/eroi/

31. David J. Murphy & Charles A.S. Hall 'Year in Review – EROI or Energy Return on (Energy) Invested', *Annals of the New York Academy of Sciences*, Volume 1185 (January 2010).

32. DOE Office of Petroleum Reserves *Fact Sheet: Energy Efficiency of Strategic Unconventional Resources*. Available from: http://fossil.energy. gov/programs/reserves/npr/Energy_Efficiency_Fact_Sheet.pdf

33. Charles A.S. Hall, Stephen Balogh & David J.R. Murphy 'What is the Minimum EROI that a Sustainable Society Must Have?' *Energies*, Volume 2, Issue 1 (2009). Available from: http://www.mdpi.com/1996-1073/2/1/25

34. David Murphy *The Energy Return on Investment Threshold*, TheOilDrum.com (25 November 2011). Available from: http://www. theoildrum.com/node/8625

35. The Sustainable Scale Project *How is Energy Scale a Problem?* (Santa Barbara Family Foundation, 2003). Available from: http:// www.sustainablescale.org/areasofconcern/Energy/EnergyandScale/ ScaleProblem.aspx

36. ENERDATA 'World Energy Expenditures', *The Global Community for Energy Professionals* (28 November 2011). Available from: http:// www.leonardo-energy.org/world-energy-expenditures

37. John Michael Greer *The Long Descent* (Gabriola Island, BC: New Society Publishers, 2008).

38. Jay Hanson *From Capitalism to Democracy: From Complexity to Simplicity* (22 May 2012). Available from: http://dieoff.org/

39. Kira Supplies Limited *Ecoware – The Greenest Multiseat Computing Solution* (2012). Available from: http://www.kira.co.uk/ecoware-the-ultimate-green-pc

40. Donella H. Meadows, Dennis L. Meadows, Jorgen Randers and William W. Behrens III *The Limits to Growth: A Report for the Club of Rome's Project on the Predicament of Mankind* (New York: Universe Books, 1972).

41. British Gas *Solar Thermal* (2012). Available from: http://www. britishgas.co.uk/products-and-services/boilers-and-central-heating/new-boilers/boiler-and-heating-range/solar-thermal.html

42. Energy Savings Trust *Ground Source Heat Pumps* (2012). Available from: http://www.energysavingtrust.org.uk/Generate-your-own-energy/ Ground-source-heat-pumps

43. Anaerobic Digestion *What is AD?* (2012). Available from: http:// www.biogas-info.co.uk/index.php/ad-basics

44. Brandon Keim 'Piezoelectric Nanowires Turn Fabric Into Power

Source', *Wired* (13 February 2008). Available from: http://www.wired. com/wiredscience/2008/02/piezoelectric-n/

45.   John Michael Greer *The Long Descent* (Gabriola Island, BC: New Society Publishers, 2008).

46.   John Michael Greer, ibid.

47.   Rob Hopkins & Peter Lipman *The Transition Network: Who We Are and What We Do . . . Version 1.0* (1 February 2009). Available from: http://www.transitionnetwork.org/resources/who-we-are-and-what-we-do

48.   Rob Hopkins & Peter Lipman, ibid.

49.   Transition Network *Wind and Democracy* (2012). Available from: http://www.transitionnetwork.org/stories/jay-tompt/2012-02/wind-and-democracy

50.   World Commission on Environment and Development *Our Common Future* (Oxford: Oxford University Press, 1987). Available from: http://www.un-documents.net/our-common-future.pdf

51.   Masdar City *What is Masdar City?* (2012). Available from: http://www.masdarcity.ae/en/27/what-is-masdar-city-/

52.   Pat Murphy *Low Energy Lifestyles: Lessons from Cuba* (Post Carbon Institute, 6 February 2005). Available from: http://www.energybulletin. net/node/4273

CHAPTER 3: DEMATERIALIZATION

53.   James Surowiecki 'Technology and Happiness', *Technology Review*, Volume 108, Issue 1. (January 2005).

54.   Intel *Advancing Sustainability Through Technology* (2007). Available from: http://www.intel.com/technology/docs/whitepaper_sustainability. pdf

55.   Intel, ibid.

56.   Dennis Pamlin & Katalin Szomolányi *Saving the Climate @ the Speed of Light* (European Telecommunications Network Operators' Association and WWF, 2006). Available from: http://www.etno. be/Portals/34/ETNO%20Documents/Sustainability/Climate%20 Change%20Road%20Map.pdf

57.   Stephanie Botelho 'Report: Tablet Sales to Cut Magazine Paper Use 20 Percent by 2015' *Folio* (22 August 2011). Available from: http://www. foliomag.com/2011/report-tablet-sales-cut-magazine-paper-use-20-percent-2015

58.   Zoe Wood 'Waterstones Deal with Amazon puts Kindle and ebooks instore' *The Guardian* (21 May 2012). Available from: http://www. guardian.co.uk/books/2012/may/21/amazon-kindle-ebook-instore

59.   Brian Heater 'Barnes & Noble Launches Instore Nook Stations', *Engadget* (7 November 2011). Available from: http://www.engadget.

com/2011/11/07/barnes-and-noble-launches-in-store-nook-stations/

60. Plastic Logic *Showing the Future for a Paperless Office* (12 July 2012). Available from: http://www.plasticlogic.com/Media-Centre.htmx ?itemid=MTUwMTIwNzA3MDYwMQ==

61. David Meyer 'EU Plans to Spend Billions on Boosting Broadband Speeds' (BBC News, 15 October 2011). Available from: http://www.bbc.co.uk/news/technology-15320628

62. Mark P. McDonald & Dave Aron *Executive Summary: Reimagining IT: The 2011 CIO Agenda* (Gartner, 1 January 2011). Available from: http://www.gartner.com/id=1524714

63. BioInfoBank Library *Development of Aero Engine Component Manufacture using Laser Additive Manufacturing* (21 September 2011). Available from: http://lib.bioinfo.pl/projects/view/22292

64. Loughborough University *3D Concrete Printing: An Innovative Construction Process* (2010). Available from: http://www.buildfreeform.com

65. The SAVING Project *Project Introduction* (2012). Available from: http://www.manufacturingthefuture.co.uk/theproject

66. Freedom of Creation *Janne Kyttanen Interviewed by Shapeways* (March 2010). Available from: http://www.freedomofcreation.com/home/janne-kyttanen-interviewed-by-shapeways

67. Mark Fleming *Fujifilm Considers Installing Thousands of 3D Printing Kiosks at Retailers* (3DPrinter.net, 3 June 2012). Available from: http://www.3dprinter.net/fujifilm-considers-3d-printing-kiosks

68. Niall Hedderman *Digging a Hole in the Ground* (Niall Hedderman, May 2012).

69. Christopher Barnatt *Valueware: Technology, Humanity and Organization* (Westport, CT: Praeger, 1999).

70. Christopher Barnatt, ibid.

71. United Nations High Level Panel on Global Sustainability *Resilient People Resilient Planet: A Future Worth Choosing* (January 2012). Available from: http://www.un.org/gsp/sites/default/files/attachments/GSP_Report_web_final.pdf

72. John Michael Greer *The Long Descent* (Gabriola Island, BC: New Society Publishers, 2008).

CHAPTER 4: DESIGN FOR REPAIR

73. Core77 *Design for [Your] Product Lifetime* (9 July 2012). Available from: http://www.core77.com/blog/design_for_your_product_lifetime

74. Freecycle *Homepage* (2012). Available from: http://www.freecycle.org/

75. Michael Braungart & William McDonough *Cradle to Cradle: Re-Making the Way We Make Things* (London: Vintage, 2009).

76.   Robert Lilienfeld & William Rathje *Use Less Stuff: Environmental Solutions for Who we Really Are* (New York: Ballantine Books, 1988).
77.   Michael Braungart & William McDonough *Cradle to Cradle: Re-Making the Way we Make Things* (London: Vintage, 2009).
78.   Autodesk *Design for Repair and Upgrade* (2012). Available from: http://sustainabilityworkshop.autodesk.com/video-script-design-repair-and-upgrade
79.   Alex Diener *Afterlife: An Essential Guide to Design for Disassembly* (Core77, 1 February 2010). Available from: http://www.core77.com/blog/featured_items/afterlife_an_essential_guide_to_design_for_disassembly_by_alex_diener__15799.asp
80.   Mister Jalopy 'Owner's Manifesto: The Maker's Bill of Rights', *MAKE Magazine* (December 2006). Available from: http://makezine.com/04/ownyourown/
81.   Patently Apple *Apple Considers a New iOS Device Design for Easier Repairs* (20 October 2011). Available from: http://www.patentlyapple.com/patently-apple/2011/10/apple-considers-a-new-ios-device-design-for-easier-repairs.html
82.   Research Council for Automobile Repairs *RCAR Design Guide: A Manufacturers' Guide to Ensure Good Design Practice for Repairability and Limitation of Damage* (August 2008). Available from: http://www.rcar.org/Papers/Design%20Guides/DesignGuide_v1_1.pdf
83.   Mike Elam *Design for Repair* (British Design Innovation, 17 May 2012). Available from: http://www.britishdesigninnovation.com/?id=2777
84.   Mike Elam, ibid.
85.   Self Storage Guide *The Self Storage Industry* (2012). Available from: http://www.self-storage.org.uk/the-self-storage-industry/

CHAPTER 5: CROWDSOURCING

86.   Jeoff Howe 'The Rise of Crowdsourcing', *Wired* (14 June 2006). Available from: http://www.wired.com/wired/archive/14.06/crowds.html
87.   'Crowdsourcing' *Merriam Webster Dictionary* (2012). Available from: http://www.merriam-webster.com/dictionary/crowdsourcing
88.   Molly Petrilla *Q&A: Britta Riley, Windowfarms Founder and R&DIY Champion* (16 April 2012). Available from: http://www.smartplanet.com/blog/pure-genius/q-a-britta-riley-windowfarms-founder-and-r-diy-champion/7973
89.   Windowfarms *The Windowfarms Project* (9 March 2010). Video available from: http://www.youtube.com/watch?v=PkCuPrsPn_I
90.   Apache OpenOffice *About Apache OpenOffice* (2012). Available from: http://www.openoffice.org/about/
91.   Apache OpenOffice, ibid.

92. Robin Wauters *300,000,000 Downloads Later, OpenOffice Ships Version 3.2* (11 February 2010). Available from: http://techcrunch.com/2010/02/11/openoffice/

93. Angus Kidman '75% of Linux Code Now Written by Paid Developers' *APC Mag* (20 January 2010). Available from: http://apcmag.com/linux-now-75-corporate.htm

94. The Linux Foundation *About Us* (2012). Available from: http://www.linuxfoundation.org/about

95. Bas van Abel, Roel Klaassen, Lucas Evers & Peter Troxler (eds) *Open Design Now* (Amsterdam: BIS Publishers, 2011). See also http://opendesignnow.org/

96. RepRap *Welcome to RepRap.org* (2012). Available from: http://reprap.org/wiki/Main_Page

97. Fab@Home *What are the Goals of the Fab@Home?* (28 July 2009). Available from: http://www.fabathome.org/?q=node/14

98. Fab@Home *Make Anything* (2012). Available from: http://fabathome.org

99. Oscar *The Idea* (2012). Available from: http://www.theoscarproject.org/index.php?option=com_content&task=view&id=6&Itemid=18

100. Riversimple *Approach* (2010). Available from: http://www.riversimple.com/Content.aspx?key=256cb5eb-798c-4d59-ae13-851e62be595a&mode=menu

101. Riversimple, ibid.

102. 40 Fires Foundation *Get Involved* (2010). Available from: http://www.40fires.org/Wiki.jsp?page=Get%20involved

103. The Open Prosthetics Project *The Project* (2012). Available from: http://openprosthetics.org/

104. Crowdcube *How it Works* (2012). Available from: http://www.crowdcube.com/pg/how-it-works-4

105. CrowdSPRING *How it Works* (2012). Available from: http://www.crowdspring.com/how-it-works/

106. Amazon Web Services *Amazon Mechanical Turk* (2012). Available from: http://aws.amazon.com/mturk/

107. Amazon Mechanical Turk, ibid.

108. Peter Diamandis & Steven Kotler *Abundance: The Future Is Better Than You Think* (New York: The Free Press, 2012).

109. BBC News *Nottingham Riots: More Officers to Deter Disorder* (10 August 2011). Available from: http://www.bbc.co.uk/news/uk-england-nottinghamshire-14480004

110. John Michael Greer *The Long Descent* (Gabriola Island, BC: New Society Publishers, 2008).

111. James Manyika, Michael Chui, Brad Brown, Jacques Bughin, Richard Dobbs, Charles Roxburgh & Angela Hung Byers *Big Data: The Next Frontier for Innovation, Competition and Productivity* (McKinsey Global

Institute, June 2011). Available from: http://www.mckinsey.com/~/media/McKinsey/dotcom/Insights%20and%20pubs/MGI/Research/Technology%20and%20Innovation/Big%20Data/MGI_big_data_full_report.ashx

112. James Manyika *et al*, ibid.

113. Jason Hiner 'US Government Commits Big R&D Money to Big Data', *ZDNet* (29 March 2012). Available from: http://www.zdnet.com/blog/btl/u-s-government-commits-big-r-and-d-money-to-big-data/72760

114. Kevin Kelly *What Technology Wants* (New York: Penguin, 2010).

115. Alice Chan 'Citroën Crowdsources its Next Car Design on Facebook' *PSKF* (6 April 2012). Available from: http://www.psfk.com/2012/04/citroen-facebook-ca.html#ixzz21vngd7Fx

CHAPTER 6: MORE WOMEN IN AUTHORITY

116. Clare Davidson *The Future is Female, BT Predicts* (BBC News, 23 April 2007). Available from: http://news.bbc.co.uk/1/hi/business/6518241.stm

117. Daniel Burrus 'The Growing Power of Women in Business', *Huffington Post* (15 February 2012). Available from: http://www.huffingtonpost.com/daniel-burrus/the-growing-power-of-wome_b_1277259.html

118. Barbara Stcherbatcheff *Confessions of a City Girl* (London: Virgin Books, 2009).

119. Barbara Stcherbatcheff, ibid.

120. US Finance Biz *Who Caused the Credit Crunch* (26 March 2009). Available from: http://usafinancebiz.com/who-caused-the-credit-crunch-men-and-their-testosterone.shtml

121. 20-First *The WOMEN-omics Special Report on the Credit Crunch: Interview with Anna Cecilie Holst.* Available from: http://www.20-first.com/411-0-credit-crunch-report-anna-cecilie-holst.html#

122. Anne Hornung-Soukup *Lessons from the Financial Crash: We Need More Women in Charge* (20-First, undated). Available from: http://www.20-first.com/405-0-what-a-fine-mess.html

123. European Commission *More Women in Senior Positions – Key to Economic Stability and Growth* (Luxembourg: Publications Office of the European Union, 2010). Available from: http://www.afaemme.org/docs/More_Women_in_Senior_Positions-Key_to_Eco_Stability&Growth_2010.pdf

124. Anne Hornung-Soukup *Lessons from the Financial Crash: We Need More Women in Charge* (20-First, undated). Available from: http://www.20-first.com/405-0-what-a-fine-mess.html

125. European Commission *More Women in Senior Positions –*

Key to Economic Stability and Growth (Luxembourg: Publications Office of the European Union, 2010). Available from: http://www.afaemme.org/docs/More_Women_in_Senior_Positions-Key_to_Eco_Stability&Growth_2010.pdf

126. Coren L. Apicella, Anna Dreber, Benjamin Campbell, Peter B. Gray, Moshe Hoffman & Anthony C. Little 'Testosterone and Financial Risk Preferences', *Evolution & Human Behaviour* Volume 29, Issue 6 (November 2008).

127. Jordan Lite 'Is Testosterone to Blame for the Financial Crisis?', *Scientific American* (30 September 2008). Available from: http://www.scientificamerican.com/blog/post.cfm?id=is-testosterone-to-blame-for-the-fi-2008-09-30

128. Anne Hornung-Soukup *Lessons from the Financial Crash: We Need More Women in Charge* (20-First, undated). Available from: http://www.20-first.com/405-0-what-a-fine-mess.html

129. *Scientific American* 'Stock Market Winners Get Big Payoff – In Testosterone' (21 April 2008). Available from: http://www.scientificamerican.com/podcast/episode.cfm?id=71A2DE32-A0B3-D4CC-9589E741CCEC9431

130. Barbara Stcherbatcheff *Confessions of a City Girl* (London: Virgin Books, 2009).

131. 20-First.com *Womenomics: Why?* (no date). Available from: http://20-first.com/2-0-why.html

132. 20-First.com, ibid.

133. Joanna Barsh & Lareina Yee 'Changing Companies' Minds About Women', *McKinsey Quarterly* (September 2011). Available from: https://www.mckinseyquarterly.com/Organization/Talent/Changing_companies_minds_about_women_2858

134. Daniel Burrus 'The Growing Power of Women in Business' *Huffington Post* (15 February 2012). Available from: http://www.huffingtonpost.com/daniel-burrus/the-growing-power-of-wome_b_1277259.html

135. Georges Desvaux, Sandrine Devillard-Hoellinger & Pascal Baumgarten *Women Matter: Gender Diversity, a Corporate Performance Driver* (McKinsey & Company, 2007). Available from: http://www.europeanpwn.net/files/mckinsey_2007_gender_matters.pdf

136. Catalyst *Companies With More Women Board Directors Experience Higher Financial Performance* (Press release, 1 October 2007). Available from: http://www.catalyst.org/press-release/73/companies-with-more-women-board-directors-experience-higher-financial-performance-according-to-latest-catalyst-bottom-line-report

137. M. Bhogaita 'Companies with a better track record of promoting women deliver superior investment performance', *New Model Advisor* (2011).

138. Goldman Sachs & JBWere Investment Research *Australia's Hidden*

Resource: The Economic Case For Increasing Female Participation (26 November 2009). Available from: http://www.eowa.gov.au/Pay_Equity/Files/Australias_hidden_resource.pdf

139. Grant Thornton 'Women in Senior Management: Still Not Enough' *Grant Thornton International Business Report* (2012). Available from: http://www.gti.org/files/ibr2012%20-%20women%20in%20senior%20management%20master.pdf

140. Grant Thornton, ibid.

141. Grant Thornton, ibid.

142. Joanna Barsh & Lareina Yee 'Changing Companies' Minds About Women', *McKinsey Quarterly* (September 2011). Available from: https://www.mckinseyquarterly.com/Organization/Talent/Changing_companies_minds_about_women_2858

143. Georges Desvaux, Sandrine Devillard-Hoellinger & Pascal Baumgarten *Women Matter: Gender Diversity, a Corporate Performance Driver* (McKinsey & Company, 2007). Available from: http://www.europeanpwn.net/files/mckinsey_2007_gender_matters.pdf

144. Joanna Barsh & Lareina Yee 'Changing Companies' Minds About Women' *McKinsey Quarterly* (September 2011). Available from: https://www.mckinseyquarterly.com/Organization/Talent/Changing_companies_minds_about_women_2858

145. Joanna Barsh & Lareina Yee, ibid.

146. Joanna Barsh & Lareina Yee, ibid.

147. Catalyst *Increasing Gender Diversity on Boards: Current Index of Formal Approaches* (2 April 2012). Available from: http://www.catalyst.org/file/532/approaches%20to%20increasing%20gender%20diversity%20on%20boards-aprilfinal.pdf

148. 2020 Women on Boards *About Us* (2012). Available from: http://www.2020wob.com/about

149. Department of Business, Innovation & Skills *Women on Boards* (February 2011). Available from: http://www.bis.gov.uk/assets/biscore/business-law/docs/w/11-745-women-on-boards.pdf

150. BBC News *Saudi Woman to be Lashed for Defying Driving Ban* (27 September 2011). Available from: http://www.bbc.co.uk/news/world-middle-east-15079620

CHAPTER 7: THE DEATH OF ECONOMICS

151. Martin Wroe *Are We There Yet? How to Tell When You've in Paradise* (Greenbelt, 2012). Video presentation available from: http://www.greenbelt.org.uk/media/video/17354-martin-wroe/

152. Paramount Pictures *Star Trek: First Contact* (1996).

153. David Suzuki *The Legacy: An Elder's Vision for Our Sustainable Future* (Vancouver, BC: Greystone, 2010).

154. David Suzuki, ibid.

155. Graeme Maxton *The End of Progress: How Modern Economics Has Failed Us* (Singapore: John Wiley & Sons, 2011).

156. Graeme Maxton, ibid.

157. Fritz Schumacher *Small Is Beautiful: Economics as if People Mattered* (London: Blond & Briggs, 1973).

158. Nicholas Stern *The Economics of Climate Change: The Stern Review* (London: HMSO Publications, 2006).

159. James Lovelock *The Vanishing Face of Gaia* (London: Allen Lane, 2009).

160. Tamra Gilbertson & Oscar Reyes *Carbon Trading: How it Works and Why it Fails* (Uppsala: Dag Hammarskjöld Foundation, 2009). Available from: http://www.carbontradewatch.org/publications/carbon-trading-how-it-works-and-why-it-fails.html

161. Tamra Gilbertson & Oscar Reyes, ibid.

162. Jos Debelke *Written Statement to Hearing by the Senate Committee on Finance on 'Auctioning under Cap and Trade: Design, Participation and Distribution of Revenues'*, (7 May 2009).

163. Peter North *Local Money: How to Make it Happen in Your Community* (Devon: Green Books, 2010).

164. The Brixton Pound *What is the B£?* (no date). Available from: http://brixtonpound.org/what

165. Bristol Pound *September 19th Launch Data Announced* (5 July 2012). Available from: http://bristolpound.org/news?id=4

166. Dan O'Neill, Rob Dietz & Nigel Jones (eds) *Enough Is Enough: Ideas for a Sustainable Economy in a World of Finite Resources. The Report of the Steady State Economy Conference.* (Arlington, VA: Center for the Advancement of the Steady State Economy, 2010). Available from: http://steadystate.org/enough-is-enough/

167. Dan O'Neill, Rob Dietz & Nigel Jones, ibid.

168. The Zeitgeist Movement *Frequently Asked Questions* (2011). Available from: http://www.thezeitgeistmovement.com/faq

169. The Zeitgeist Movement, ibid.

170. The Zeitgeist Movement *Mission Statement* (2011). Available from: http://www.thezeitgeistmovement.com/mission-statement

Epilogue

171. Donella H. Meadows, Dennis L. Meadows, Jorgen Randers & William W. Behrens III *The Limits to Growth: A Report for the Club of Rome's Project on the Predicament of Mankind* (New York: Universe Books, 1972).

172. John Michael Greer *The Long Descent* (Gabriola Island, BC: New Society Publishers, 2008).

INDEX

Made in the USA
Lexington, KY
28 October 2012